Free Play
in Early
Childhood

Free Play in Early Childhood

A literature review

Childhood

Joan Santer and Carol Griffiths, with Deborah Goodall

NCB promotes the voices, interests and well-being of all children and young people across every aspect of their lives.

As an umbrella body for the children's sector in England and Northern Ireland, we provide essential information on policy, research and best practice for our members and other partners.

NCB aims to:

- challenge disadvantage in childhood
- work with children and young people to ensure they are involved in all matters that affect their lives
- promote multidisciplinary cross-agency partnerships and good practice
- influence government policy through policy development and advocacy
- undertake high quality research and work from an evidence-based perspective
- disseminate information to all those working with children and young people, and to children and young people themselves.

NCB has adopted and works within the UN Convention on the Rights of the Child.

Published by the National Children's Bureau

National Children's Bureau, 8 Wakley Street, London EC1V 7QE
Tel: 020 7843 6000
Website: www.ncb.org.uk
Registered charity number: 258825

NCB works in partnership with Children in Scotland (www.childreninscotland.org.uk) and Children in Wales (www.childreninwales.org.uk).

Play England is a project of the Children's Play Council, part of the National Children's Bureau, and is supported by the Big Lottery Fund.

© National Children's Bureau 2007

ISBN 13: 978-1-905818-10-5

British Library Cataloguing in Publication Data
A catalogue record for this book is available from the British Library.

Acknowledgements

This literature review was compiled by Joan Santer and Carol Griffiths with Deborah Goodall based at the University of Northumbria. The review was edited by Issy Cole-Hamilton.

Thanks for their support on this project in particular to Judith Anderson and Sue Owen. Also to John Alwyine-Mosely, Celia Burgess-Macey, Peta Cubberley, Julie Fisher, Chris Foster, Lydia Keyte, Paulette Luff, Paula McMahon, Ann-Marie McAuliffe, Alison Moore-Gwyn, Janni Nicol, Simon Perry, Dorothy Selleck and Stephen York.

Images supplied by:

Page ii: Photograph: Diane Stevens

Page vi: Photograph: Michael Bretherton

Page x: Photograph Janet Goulden

Page 1: Photograph: Janis Gonser

Page 21: Photograph: Janet Goulden

Page 29: Photograph: Afonso Lima

Page 45: Copyright Anissa Thompson, www.anissat.com/photos.php

Page 59: Copyright Anissa Thompson, www.anissat.com/photos.php

Joan Santer

Joan Santer is Senior Lecturer at Northumbria University. She is leader of the Childhood Studies route, which is part of the BA Joint Honours Programme. She also works as an independent trainer, consultant and researcher into early childhood.

Joan previously worked at the University of Newcastle, as Director of the Early Childhood Studies degree programme. She was also, for a number of years, a teacher of infant and nursery children, and an advisor to statutory and voluntary pre-school providers in a local education authority.

Joan's research activity focuses predominantly upon the early childhood curriculum and child autonomy.

Carol Griffiths

Carol Griffiths (formerly Buswell) is a sociologist at Northumbria University. She has researched and published across a wide range of issues including aspects of inequality, education, training, employment and Sure Start programmes. She is currently working on urban regeneration projects that will facilitate, and take account of, 'children's voices'.

Deborah Goodall

Deborah Goodall graduated from Loughborough University in 1987 with a First Class Honours degree in Library and Information Studies. She then worked at the University's Library and Statistics Unit, and published papers on browsing in public libraries and performance measurement. Deborah subsequently became Lecturer in the Department of Library Studies at Loughborough University.

Deborah completed her PhD in 1999. She currently works part-time as an Information Specialist and a Research Associate at Northumbria University. Deborah has a keen interest in research methods.

On 20 November 1989 the United Nations Convention on the Rights of the Child was adopted by the UN General Assembly, it was ratified by the UK government in 1991. The convention places a responsibility on governments to work for 'their own' and for the world's children (Newell 1993). It contains a number of articles that declare internationally accepted principles. Under Article 31 of the Convention: 'States parties recognize the right of the child to rest and leisure, to engage in play and recreational activities appropriate to the age of the child and to participate freely in cultural life and the arts.' The countries belonging to the United Nations, therefore, have recognised play as a right for all children. The importance of this right is nowhere more important than in the lives of very young children.

This literature review focuses on free play in early childhood. Play such as 'planned play' is also referred to. Where the term 'play' is used, it refers to free play unless stated otherwise. The term 'early years' encompasses children from birth to 7 years.

The literature review contains the following chapters:

1. *Perspectives on play* gives an historical and modern perspective on understanding and policy relating to children's play.
2. *Play, exploration and brain development* draws on a range of perspectives, examines the relationship between play, exploration and brain development, and shows the interdependence of these aspects of development.
3. *Play, development and learning* focuses on emotional, social, intellectual and physical development.
4. *Play-related themes* discusses a range of issues that permeate understanding free play.
5. *Role of the adult* focuses on the complex role that adults play in supporting children's play.
6. *Discussion* highlights the main findings in the literature, the issues they bring to light, and poses some questions for reflection.

This literature review, focusing on free play in early childhood (from birth to 7 years old), was commissioned by Play England, and the work was carried out between May and July 2006. Its aim is to provide information about the value of free play in early childhood.

Free play is described by Play England as:

> … children choosing what they want to do, how they want to do it and when to stop and try something else. Free play has no external goals set by adults and has no adult imposed curriculum. Although adults usually provide the space and resources for free play and might be involved, the child takes the lead and the adults respond to cues from the child.

The concept of choice is crucial to an understanding of play and play provision. This does not imply an absence of boundaries. It does imply that these boundaries are managed within a primary consideration of the child's need to choose its own play.

Methodology

The body of literature concerning free play is vast, with perspectives provided from distinctly different disciplines and undertaken with different degrees of academic rigour. This literature review draws on a range of viewpoints, including observational studies, the work of pioneers and well-respected writers in the field, as well as research-based studies. In doing so, it provides insights from different professional contexts, types of early years provision and theoretical perspectives.

Data were collected by accessing databases and using internet searches (see Appendix A). Frameworks detailing the type of literature, its themes and insights, methods, findings and conclusions were created for managing and analysing the data.

Priority was given to articles in refereed journals because these had undergone peer scrutiny. Every effort was made during the writing of the review to provide information regarding the methodology of research in a manner that did not interfere with the coherence of the text.

The search fields constrained the data in that some articles focused on children from birth to 3 years old, but the majority reflected the experiences of children from 3–5 years of age. There was a dearth of information on free play for children aged from 5–7 years. We believe, however, that this reflects a trend across literature in general.

The literature in this review is predominantly from the United Kingdom. This ensured that the review was both manageable and relevant to the audience for which it has been written – those who work with young children in England.

Perspectives on play

Since the early philosophers, people have been writing intermittently about children's play. Over time, the focus has moved from attempts to describe it to efforts to understand what children do when they are playing, and indeed the links between this and their development and learning.

Play has been given some visibility in recent legislation and guidance, as research findings have identified it as an indicator of high quality provision. However, the concept of play is ill-defined in current government documentation.

The extent to which play has been valued in the early years curriculum has changed over time. Recent research has shown that there is a tension between the ideology and practice of early years practitioners in relation to play. This has been attributed to an overemphasis on attainment targets and testing.

Play in children's development

Children are highly motivated to play, although adults find defining and understanding children's play a challenge. All aspects of development and learning are related in play, particularly the affective and cognitive domains. When children have time to play, their play grows in complexity and becomes more cognitively and socially demanding. Through free play children:
- explore materials and discover their properties
- use their knowledge of materials to play imaginatively
- express their emotions and reveal their inner feelings
- come to terms with traumatic experiences
- maintain emotional balance, physical and mental health, and well-being
- struggle with issues such as birth and death, good and evil, and power and powerlessness
- develop a sense of who they are, their value and that of others
- learn social skills of sharing, turn-taking and negotiation
- deal with conflict and learn to negotiate
- solve problems, moving from support to independence
- develop communication and language skills
- repeat patterns that reflect their prevailing interests and concerns

- use symbols as forms of representation – the use of symbols is crucial in the development from learning through the senses to the development of abstract thought
- practise, develop and master skills across all aspects of development and learning.

Children today have fewer opportunities for outdoor play than their predecessors. Environments for outdoor play are generally underutilised and the role of the adult in this is frequently passive.

In play children seek out risks, because through these they develop their self-esteem and confidence. They need physically challenging experiences. Risk is an intelligent behaviour. Adult caution and fear reduce children's opportunities to set themselves challenges and take risks.

Recurring themes in play

Throughout the literature on play there are a number of recurring themes.

Gender

Girls and boys from the age of three tend to seek out same-sex play partners, and this behaviour increases over time. The play of boys and girls is generally different. Boys engage in more forceful and aggressive play than girls. Boys are more likely to be in larger groups, girls in dyads when they play. There also appears to be a relationship between more frequent play with same-sex peers and gender stereotyped behaviour.

Children's voices

Children are infrequently consulted concerning their play experiences, environments, and the materials and resources to support these. When they have been asked, children have reported that friendships, opportunities for play and choices within their play are vital to them. Children in early years settings enjoy play would like more choice in what they do, and when they play, particularly in relation to outdoor play.

Play and culture

The concept of play in other parts of the UK and other countries, such as Wales, Italy and Scandinavian countries, tends to be based on images of children as strong individuals who are actively engaged in their own learning, and who also have the right to have their voices heard on all issues concerning them.

Inclusion

Some groups of children are excluded either overtly or covertly from participating fully in play because of ethnicity, lifestyle, disability or ill-health. Exclusion brings serious risks to the child's social and emotional well-being. In some circumstances social exclusion may be sanctioned by groups in order to maintain their smooth functioning, so early intervention can be necessary to avoid socially aversive exchanges developing into active victimisation. Rejected children can become aggressive in response to these situations.

Stressed, abused and ill children

Children who are maltreated tend to have poorer social skills than their peers. Depressed children use less symbolic play and move more frequently between types of play. This may be because symbolic play can be threatening due to its potential to raise negative thoughts and feelings. Mood inhibits the child's play and the capacity of children to respond creatively within their daily interactions can be constrained by the psychological environment.

Children who are preoccupied and anxious may be unable to play, and therefore can be deprived of active and safe means of problem solving.

Providing ill children with more play opportunities may improve the quality of their health.

Disabled children

Some children are not able to explore their environments and the materials within them. They are, therefore, unable to gather information through their senses and movement. Dependency on caregivers, time required for therapy and tiredness of carers may reduce the opportunities that children who are disabled have for play. Dependency on others can become a secondary disability. Limited interaction results in limited social skills. In this context adults are crucial in choosing appropriate materials, ensuring time for play, and supporting the child in initiating and sustaining play sessions.

Fostering inclusion

All children should participate to their fullest in play. Children who are disabled tend to spend more time in solitary play than 'typically developing' children. The latter include others with disabilities when they understand the constraints of the disability, and the implications of this for play. The repetitive, isolated play of children with severe disorders can be extended through focused interventions.

Children need time to repeat, practise and rehearse their play. Daily routines and timetables should be flexible enough to accommodate these processes.

Role of the adult

Although free play is by definition child-led, adults have a crucial role in providing suitable environments and in facilitating children's experiences.

Sensitivity and attachment

In order to support and extend children's play, the adult must develop a repertoire of responses that are appropriate to each play situation and the needs of individual children. The primary role of the adult is to create both a psychologically and physically suitable context in which children feel secure, develop a sense of their worth, and that of others, and have the freedom and autonomy to explore. Cooperation, responsive interactions and 'mind-related' comments ensure that children become securely attached. Children who enjoy strong attachments with their mothers are more likely when older to be conciliatory with friends, and to enter elaborate shared fantasy bouts and conversations. Adults who are inconsistent and insensitive can, in the short term, cause psychological damage, trauma and negative self-esteem. In the long term the result may be an inability of the child to 'tune in to', or empathise with others.

Adults working with children who are disabled may need to communicate through the senses using touch, texture, music, aromatherapy, signing and body language.

Observation

Observation is a vital element of working with young children. Observation of play provides information about:

- children's interests, which in turn guide the choice of resources for the environment that will support and extend children's play
- what children do in their play
- how long they persist in play
- the patterns that emerge in their play
- partners who share their play and
- the child's affective disposition and social and linguistic skills.

Interaction

The extent to which adults interact with children during their free play will vary depending on the circumstances. Premature intervention in children's play can rob them of the opportunity to make mistakes, learn from these, solve problems creatively and negotiate solutions to social conflict. In some situations the adult should act as a non-participant in the play, in others as a play partner and in others as a talk partner.

Children who are disabled may need the adult to adopt a more structured approach. This may include supporting those who have a lack of mobility, or insufficient fine motor skills, in accessing objects, modelling play with objects, encouraging play with others to develop their social skills, and helping children to initiate and sustain their play.

Many writers assert that for all children, the adult has an active role in challenging stereotypes or anti-social behaviours that arise, both within and beyond the play situation. This must be done in a sensitive but fair way. Adults are role models for children, and therefore they have the power to influence their values, attitudes and behaviour.

The timing of interactions is crucial so that adults do not intrude upon, frustrate or terminate the child's play, but rather support and extend the play. The skill is knowing when and how to become part of the action.

The environment

Adults are responsible for choosing and storing materials and resources, based on their knowledge of child development and individual children's interests and abilities. In order to support children's exploration in play, a wide range of materials should be made available, including those that are familiar, novel, natural and open-ended. They should reflect cultural diversity. This is particularly important for children from minority groups, who, in some situations, may experience exclusion and isolation.

Resources chosen for children who are disabled should be developmentally appropriate and flexible in use; for example, things that can be held in the hands or by feet. The adult should participate as actively in the outdoor environment as in the indoor environment. Routines and timetables should be flexible in accommodating children's play in order to facilitate the move from simple to complex and cooperative play.

Familiarity with children's interests in free play can inform adult-initiated activities as well as exchanges with parents and carers. Without explanatory power, interpretation and response by adults, observations have little meaning.

Conclusions

Free play in early childhood is a vital experience through which children learn social, conceptual and creative skills, as well as increasing their knowledge and understanding of the world around them.

Free play is highly motivating and complex. Those involved in working with young children should gain the best insights possible into its meaning. However, due to its complexity, play may defy the act of definition. Although play is not the only way in which children learn, it is an essential part of their early development and learning. The benefits of play in early childhood – to children, families and communities – continue into later life, probably contributing to increased social responsibility and reduced antisocial behaviour, and to the ability to make a contribution through employment.

The Welsh Assembly Government has made an explicit commitment to free play. The Foundation Stage in Wales, which is underpinned by a play-based curriculum, includes Key Stage 1.

Some of the issues that arise in this literature review have implications for the development of our understanding of play, and indicate the need for a series of possible actions:

- If we are to ensure that children have the right to play as defined in the United Nations Convention on the Rights of the Child, 1989, there should be more emphasis on child development and the role of play, including free play, in the training of all adults working with young children.
- Local authorities and others should make it a priority to provide training that highlights the benefits of free play, and the strategies to support this, for all staff in their early years settings.
- There would be benefits in drawing together professionals such as playworkers, play therapists, occupational therapists and educationalists to share their expertise with one another and inform initial and in-service training on issues related to play.
- As more is known about the play of 3–5 year olds than older children, further research should be carried out to investigate free play experiences of children aged 5–7 years, both in their school contexts and in the community.

- Practitioners should be actively recruited as researchers on such projects because they are in the best position to understand the issues, disseminate knowledge and bring about change.
- There should be further research investigating risk-taking and play and the play experiences of children from excluded groups.
- Information and resources should be available to support small groups in the development of stimulating outdoor areas in early years settings.

One important issue for future discussion is the terminology used to describe and discuss play. A lack of shared language and understanding currently inhibits communication between those working to provide children with the best opportunities for play.

As play for all ages of children becomes increasingly a topic of debate and the subject of public policy, it can be argued that consequent developments in the services and environments that children are offered will be most effective if they are informed by a cohesive and consistent knowledge base and its attendant language. Play is perhaps too profound and intangible a concept to neatly define in a way that brooks no argument. Neverthless, it is increasingly important for all children's professionals to enter into a dialogue with, and between, play and early years' practitioners, in order to develop shared understandings and terms that best describe the theoretical bases, the aims of provision and the tenets of good practice.

History of discussion on play

Plato (in his late dialogue, *Laws*) recognised the physical nature of young children when he stated: 'The young of all creatures cannot keep their bodies still or their tongues quiet: they are always wanting to move and cry out; some are leaping and skipping and overflowing with playfulness and pleasure, and others uttering all sorts of cries.' In *The Republic* he also talked about an appropriate approach to learning for the young: 'Enforced learning will not stay in the mind. So avoid compulsion and let your children's lessons take the form of play.'

Garvey (1991) also writes of children's exuberance, regarding it as a universal characteristic of play. Present day authors would agree that it is a natural instinct for children across all cultures to play. Historically, however, play has been viewed quite differently depending on the prevailing views of children and childhood.

Cohen (1993) suggests that play is as old as mankind. He reports that archaeological evidence reveals that Greek and Roman children played with objects. Greek children were creative in making balls from pigs' bladders and Roman children used toy soldiers. They also took part in running and jumping games and piggybacked fights. Hoops were made from the iron frames of wheels in the time of Aurelius. The play of children always reflected the society in which the children lived, and, certainly in the case of Greek and Roman children, physical activities took place alongside adults. During these times, play was not considered worthy of documentation.

In the 13th century medieval art reflected the play of children, but this was only on the periphery of paintings and never as a central interest. There was also a notable absence of comment on play in literature during this period. However, by the 16th century children's games had become the focus of artists' representations. In the 17th century, diarists recorded their disregard for what was perceived to be 'trivial', which included play. John Locke, a philosopher, acknowledged that children were predisposed to be curious, but was no advocate of play, which he considered to be silly and trivial. Play, at this time, was clearly not worthy of either discussion or debate.

With the impact of the Romantic movement in the 18th century, play came to the fore and was valued. Rousseau was central to normalising this in his work *Emile* (1762/1963) which was a call back to nature, reflecting his philosophy that children should have time to explore the natural world. He believed that play was a child's right and that there was no antithesis between this and work. Play liberated children. Rousseau's philosophy stressed the importance of play as an instrument for the development of the senses, the exercise of judgement through sensory experience and contact with things: 'Let all the lessons of young children take the form of doing rather than talking, let them learn nothing from books that they can learn from experience' (Rousseau 1762/1963: 101).

Rousseau's work influenced Pestalozzi, a Swiss writer, philosopher and defender of the poor, who valued play as central to human fulfilment and achievement at each stage of development. It also affected the work of Froebel, who was German. He believed play to be fundamental to all growth. He highlighted the necessity of interconnectedness and harmony between the inner and outer worlds of the child. The role of adults was to provide environments in which children could explore 'in areas not yet known but vaguely surmised' (Liebschner 1991: 15). The environment was crucial to the child's development and learning: 'The educator only has to learn how to provide the widest opportunities and means, as well as the fullest freedom for such play' (Froebel cited in Lawrence 1952: 192).

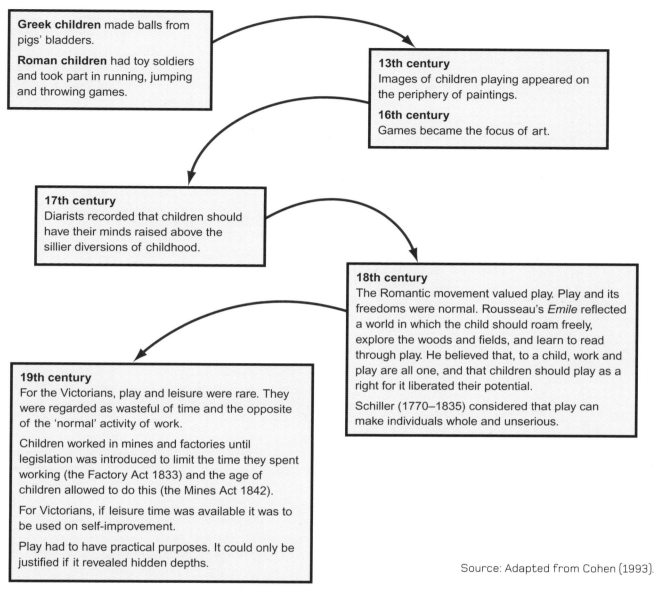

Figure 1.1 Perspectives on play over time

Similarly, Schiller (1770–1835), a German philosopher, advocated that play was a means of becoming whole and unserious. In his *Ode to Joy* he defined play as the 'aimless expenditure of exuberant energy'. This was not a popular message at the time.

In the Victorian era the change from an agrarian to an industrial economy brought a new seriousness to society. Children who had previously worked on the land were now working in the mills and factories for long hours. Play and leisure therefore were rare. Work was regarded as the norm and play was the opposite of this, therefore considered by many as wasteful of time. Such were the concerns about the experiences of children who were working long hours in unsatisfactory environments that legislation was introduced to limit the time that they spent underground (the Mines Act 1842) and the age at which they were allowed to work (the Factory Act 1833). The Victorians believed that if people had leisure time they were to use it to improve themselves. Documents of the time, however, reveal the creativity of children in finding time to punctuate their daily work with bouts of play activity (Cohen 1993). Bartoletti (1996) writes of children aged five and six working long hours in coal mines and factories in the early 1900s; however, he notes that boys sometimes jammed the machines so that they could stop and play.

We can see that the documentation of play as a phenomenon worthy of report has been relatively recent, and that attitudes towards it have changed significantly over time. From the 1870s research on play began to be of scientific interest and branched into three directions based on its cognitive, emotional and social value.

Classical and modern dynamic theories

Saracho and Spodek (1998) describe two approaches to play in the 19th and 20th centuries; classical and modern dynamic. In the classical theories the concern was to explain the *reason that play exists*. The explanations included:

- *The relaxation theory* in which individuals recharge energy that they exhaust in work. Therefore play is relaxation and a source of energy before beginning work again.
- *The surplus energy theory*, in contrast to the relaxation theory, viewed play as a means of eliminating excess energy. Play therefore was regarded as an instinctive behaviour with no immediate goal. The nineteenth century psychologist, Herbert Spencer's theory was heavily influenced by the work of Schiller in the previous century.
- *The recapitulation theory* under which individuals are believed to be going through personal development that is parallel to the experiences of the human race. Play reflects the course of evolution and is a migration through primitive stages in order to prepare for the endeavours of modern life. The work of Stanley Hall, a psychologist in the early twentieth century, is most associated with this perspective.
- *Play as pre-exercise*. According to this perspective play is an instinctive way of preparing children for adult life. Play experiences are similar to those they will experience as adults, and therefore children are rehearsing adult skills in their play. The German evolutionary biologist, Karl Groos, espoused this view in the late nineteenth century, believing play was functional and characterised by undefined activity, pleasure and dominated by

process rather than product. He believed that experimental play developed mental skills and self-control, and imitative play developed inter-personal skills.

In contrast to the classical theories, the modern dynamic perspectives seek to explain the *content* of play. The theorists central to these perspectives are Freud, Piaget and Vygotsky. Each will be discussed briefly in turn in order to set the scene for later discussion.

From the psychodynamic perspective (Freud, Erikson and Isaacs), children communicate and eliminate anxieties and fears by bringing them to a level of consciousness that can then be articulated through play. Fantasy is a means of coping with elements of reality that are difficult for children. By this means everyday problems are reduced. Within this perspective children's language in play is regarded as parallel to the language used by adults in psychoanalysis. It is a means of accessing the pre and subconscious.

One of the difficulties with this theoretical perspective is that the affective and internal processes of individuals are being evaluated by those other than the individuals themselves. The claims being made by theorists and practitioners, therefore, are difficult to validate at a 'scientific' level. This criticism made of the work of Freud still persists in some quarters today, although it could be argued that the emotional dimension of human personality is valued more highly now due to the work of writers such as Goleman (1996).

Piaget was interested in children's thinking and how this developed. He believed that children build up their knowledge through active engagement with the environment (a constructivist theory). He studied play primarily from a cognitive viewpoint. From Piaget's perspective, learning takes place through the processes of 'assimilation' and 'accommodation'. Assimilation is the taking in of new knowledge from the world and accommodation is adapting this to fit with previously developed understanding or schemas. Piaget believed that learning is a continuing process of adaptation to the environment. Piaget viewed the child's development as leading learning, with play having a strong influence on development. Therefore play has an important educational purpose. Piaget paid less attention to the role of language in learning.

Piaget's work was carried out predominantly in laboratories and through observations of his own children. As a consequence, his work can be criticised as being more theoretical than empirical (Herron and Sutton-Smith 1971). Piaget conceptualised children's development in terms of stages that occur across all cultures, although at different rates depending upon experiences. More recent work questions this stage approach. Donaldson (1978) for example provides a helpful commentary on the work of Piaget.

Vygotsky, a Russian, understood all children's learning to occur within a social context. He was a social constructivist. In his theory he placed the support of others (or scaffolding) as central to developing children's understanding. In this respect, language makes a critical contribution to the child's construction of his or her learning. The adult has a distinct role in moving children on from their present, to their potential development. In contrast to Piaget, Vygotsky understood learning to lead development. Unlike Freud he did not believe that play arises as a result of unsatisfied desires. Conversely, he believed children create play that has purpose, and which, in turn, determines their affective states. Vygotsky stated that the child's greatest achievements were possible in play because: 'In play a child behaves beyond his average age, above his daily behaviour; in play it is as though he were a head taller than himself' (Vygotsky 1978: 102). Essentially then, the child moves forward through play activity.

Wood and Attfield (1996) remind us that committing to any one theory to the exclusion of others is unwise. They recall that Vygostsky's early death mitigated against his theories being tested in depth, translation from his Russian tongue has altered his work, and contemporaries and followers have reinterpreted and synthesised his theory in the light of their subsequent insights.

In conclusion, we can see from the above discussion that theorists hold quite fundamentally different views about the nature and purposes of play. Freud regarded play as having a strong affective purpose, Piaget argued for cognitive development through play, while Vygotsky regarded imaginative play as liberating children from their immediate situational constraints. However, they all agree on one thing – that there *are* benefits for children when they play.

Play in early childhood

Within the early childhood field, there is an ongoing dialogue regarding what constitutes a 'quality' experience for young children. Ball (1994) highlighted that high quality early education, rather than type of provision, leads to lasting cognitive and social benefits, especially for economically disadvantaged children. In the same document, Sylva (1994) described the concept of quality as embracing, among other things, active learning or purposeful play. This suggests that while play is valued, writers do not regard all play as purposeful.

At the heart of the discourse about quality is the struggle to identify the interactions, contexts and experiences that best facilitate the growth and development of our young, and that will serve them best for living in an age of rapid change. In an era when services are increasingly being called to account for the quality of their provision, there is tension between what are perceived to be children's needs (usually identified by adults) and the needs of society with regard to the skills and competencies required in the future workforce. This is even more the case since closer relationships with Europe have brought to our attention comparisons between different cultural values, beliefs and children's academic achievements and later success in society. There is, for some, a dichotomy between work and play; the former being valued and the latter regarded as trivial and inconsequential.

Play is clearly a difficult concept to define. As Moyles (2005: 4) states: 'Grappling with the concept of play is analogous to trying to seize bubbles, for every time there appears to be something to hold on to, its ephemeral nature disallows it being grasped.' It is perhaps more helpful to consider play as a process that embraces a wide range of behaviours, skills, motivations and opportunities. Moyles (2005) regards play as a multifaceted layer of activities.

More than one meaning can be attached to play. Like a diamond, it has many different facets, and the angle from which it is observed determines the nature of the image that is reflected. The same can be said of the perspectives of theorists, who inevitably bring with them their culture, professional heritage and underlying values and beliefs, which become the filter through which they study play.

Early pioneers in early childhood studies such as Froebel, Montessori and Steiner, who were influenced by the work of Rousseau, were in turn instrumental in influencing thinking regarding the early years curriculum. They all believed that childhood is a distinctly different state from adulthood and that adults therefore should not seek to prepare children for adulthood. Froebel moved away from his earlier set curriculum to a position where he saw play as a means of maintaining the wholeness of experience. Play was a unifying mechanism. Froebel, Montessori and Steiner all believed children were self-motivating and highly intrinsically motivated. They also believed that adults had a tendency to be too dominant and cut across this motivation. Montessori, however, did not believe in play or toys. Children in her kindergartens experienced real household tasks. Froebel believed that children were strong and confident and that through play they saw things through to completion.

Following close observations of children, another early years pioneer, Susan Isaacs (1932), noted that the following developed through spontaneous play:

- love of movement and perfecting bodily skills

- interest in actual things and events – the discovery of the world without
- delight in make-believe and the expression of the world within.

At the beginning of the 20th century, sisters Margaret and Rachel Macmillan were concerned about children's health and were strong advocates of fresh air and play in the outdoor environment. Development of the imagination was also central to their philosophy. In 1914 the sisters established an open-air nursery school and training centre in Peckham. Margaret Macmillan criticised the government of the day for opening schools in working class areas that concentrated on preparing children for unskilled and monotonous jobs instead of offering a broad and humane education.

We are given a fascinating insight into education in the 1930s in the work of Ella Ruth Boyce (1938) who was a teacher in an infants' school in Stepney, London, a disadvantaged area where many children possessed no toys. The school was moving from a formal to a more child-centred approach. Boyce describes giving children half of each day with selected materials and minimum interference to play in their own way. If problems arose, adult and child solved them together. The principle of 'activity as a means of learning' guided these sessions. There was no antithesis between work and play. Some areas of the environment were screened off to give children space for construction and cooperative work. Boyce makes explicit the rationale: 'We insisted that the children should not be made to fit into any school machinery, but that the machinery could be altered to fit them' (Boyce 1938: 19).

Although at first there were some difficulties regarding the children's behaviour, as the staff persevered they discovered that the more freedom they gave the children the richer their personalities were. Children also responded more to the environment that had been provided. The imaginative nature of their play was particularly pronounced. As the children were responding, so the staff were gaining benefits: 'In spite of many anxious times of hard work and temporary disappointment, we felt that the children were sweeping us along with their interests and their living experiences; we were fulfilling our purposes because they fulfilled so many of their own' (Boyce 1938: 185).

It is clear that play has frequently been an area of debate, and the extent to which it should be central to children's experience and learning widely discussed. When state funded nursery education was halted in the 1960s the Preschool Playgroups Association (which subsequently became the Preschool Learning Alliance in 1995) was formed by parents frustrated by the lack of provision. This movement grew rapidly and was responsible for the prolific increase in writing and training on play-based provision.

In the late 1990s interest arose concerning the type of setting that can best foster children's development and learning. In their work based on the Child Health and Education Study of 8,400 children born in 1970, Osborn and Milbank (1987) declared that play with peers, plus proper care and interesting experiences rather than type of provision, should be fundamental to the experience of young children.

The insightful Rumbold report (Department of Education and Science 1990) recorded that children need talk, play and first-hand experiences because these are powerful in the child's development and learning. More recently the Effective Provision of Preschool Education Project (EPPE), following 3,000 children from the age of three plus to the end of Key Stage 1, has explored the impact of preschool on children's intellectual and social/behavioural development and sought to identify characteristics of effective preschool settings. According to Sylva and others (2004: vi): 'EPPE concludes that in most effective centres "play" environments were used to provide the basis of instructive learning. However the most effective pedagogy combine both "teaching" and providing freely chosen yet potentially instructive play activities ... freely chosen play activities often provided the best opportunities for adults to extend children's thinking.'

It is clear that in relation to the early years curriculum, play and learning are closely connected, the latter being fostered by the former.

We are informed by research that there are some dichotomies within early years practice. There is a tension between the language of play and the extent to which adults understand its true potential and, indeed, are able to translate their understanding into an effective pedagogy. For example Wood and Attfield (1996) highlight that not all children have the opportunity to learn through play and not all practitioners know how to teach through play. Bennett and Kell (1989), who observed children in reception classes, had previously reported that teachers often planned to be involved in adult-directed activities with small groups of children, while children initiating their own play activities were left unsupported in their play. Children may, as a result, receive the message that some activities are more important than others; most specifically, that what adults do is more important than what children choose to do. We may conclude, therefore, that in some situations there is a lack of confidence in play as a primary means of learning.

A further issue for those working in the early years is concern regarding the increasing emphasis on attainment targets for young children, and the extent to which this impacts on the nature of the curriculum, making it more directive and outcomes-oriented.

According to (Lansdown and Lancaster 2001: 42): 'There is a serious cause for concern that the current emphasis on attainment targets for preschool children will jeopardise their opportunities for play.'

Hendy and Whitebread (2000) investigated interpretations of children from nursery through to Year 2, and perceptions of parents and teachers concerning independent learning. They explored the extent to which these interpretations influenced classroom planning and practice. They found that children at aged three were able to express choices and preferences and describe their own abilities and difficulties; older children were able to recognise the learning that they had achieved. This message will be no surprise to those who have close relationships with young children. Furthermore, the research found that parents had a more rounded concept of children's independence than teachers. Parents emphasised the abilities of children in areas of self-help, social development and personal development. In contrast, teachers were concerned with organisational aspects of independence rather than physical, social or cognitive benefits. Neither parents nor teachers emphasised cognitive independence through independent learning. Children's abilities to think and act independently were underestimated by teachers particularly at the older end of the age range. Nursery children were likely to solve problems themselves, older children (particularly those in reception class) were inclined to involve adults. Children became more teacher-dependent in the first years at school. It appears that in schools a dependency culture may be created as children get older. In their report Hendy and Whitebread provide no details of the initial or post-qualifying training of the teachers in the study. However, these insights prompt us to consider the content of initial teacher training and the extent to which it impacts on classroom practice. Are links between play, pedagogy (the principles and practice of teaching) and learning made explicit?

Recent literature

The booklet *Qualifying to Teach: Handbook of Guidance* (Teacher Training Agency 2003) contains the outcomes, or professional standards, for initial teacher training providers. Standard S2.1a highlights requirements trainees must possess before entering into the teaching profession. It states (at page 15) that they must be able to 'support and extend children's play, learning and development' in the Foundation Stage. However, no further guidance is given on the issue and little is said about play, either in the other standards or in relation to teaching beyond the Foundation Stage.

A recent study by Adams and others (2004), commissioned by the Association of Teachers and Lecturers (ATL), sought to discover how the introduction of the Foundation Stage for children aged 3–5 years was changing practice in school reception classes. The researchers undertook the project over a 15-month period between March 2002 and May 2003. The work was carried out in 11 local authorities in England.

This research details the difference between rhetoric and reality in the early years, with teachers feeling unable to provide a curriculum they prefer due to pressures to perform in tests, performance tables and targets. The authors state that practitioners still feel the need to justify play and its inclusion in the curriculum. As in the work of Hendy and Whitebread (2000), practitioners were found to be unsure of the relationship between play and cognitive development and seemed to lack a theoretical underpinning of reception class pedagogy. Half were unaware of the pedagogy of theorists Piaget and Vygotsky, and many recorded that their practice was influenced and informed by their own experience, school approaches and documentation.

Although staff in this piece of research recorded in their questionnaire responses that they regarded outdoor play as essential, and that they placed a high value on learning through play, in reality there was a tension between children having time to play and teachers having time to teach. These were seen as two distinct aspects, rather than complementary experiences. The reception year teachers were influenced more by the challenges of Year 1 than the nursery curriculum. Although they emphasised independent learning, they worried whether children would meet targets, specifically those for literacy and numeracy. Thus their main focus was on teaching reading, writing and numeracy.

Observations of classroom practice revealed that children were experiencing highly structured adult-led activities of short duration, interspersed with long periods of free choice with little interaction. The authors record that both child and adult-led activities had little challenge and meaning for children.

Practice was that children played alone while teachers taught the timetable. The report indicates that the most worrying finding was the limited opportunities for sustained, shared, purposeful talk, for complex imaginative play and for authentic, engaging, first-hand experiences. Opportunities for sustained, complex play were disappointing due to the tight schedule of adult-led activities, and opportunities were missed to observe, engage with and extend play.

Many educators in the study talked unreservedly about the value of free flow play for children's learning; however, the classrooms observed showed that play was often constrained and curtailed. Sometimes this was due to issues of management; for example, in one setting outdoor play could only be accessed by one-third of the children at a time. In another classroom materials were accessible behind curtains but only when the adult lifted the curtain. Concerns regarding health and safety also limited children's experience. For example, children who were making soup had blunt knives to cut vegetables, which led to adults doing the work for them with the children losing the opportunity to use knives appropriately as a result. Children were also observed to be called away from their play activities to do adult-initiated activities. The similarity between some of these findings and those of Tizard and others (1988) working in Inner City London is both striking and worrying. Worrying particularly because of the apparent lack of improvement in provision over nearly two decades.

Adams and others (2004) recognised that warm caring relationships were fostered in the settings they observed, and that these provided a secure base for future development. However, they emphatically state that the Foundation Stage is not a preparation for formal schooling, but is a distinct and separate phase. They also remind readers that most children in Europe are not in school at this age.

Government legislation and initiatives

Over the past decade young children, families and their communities have increasingly become the centre of political attention. National organisations such as the Early Childhood Forum (formerly The Early Childhood Education Forum, established in 1993) have campaigned on behalf of young children, drawing together individuals and groups to collaborate on projects and issues of national importance regarding early childhood. In addition, they have been proactive in publishing materials such as *Quality in Diversity in Early Learning: A Framework for Early Childhood Practitioners* (Early Childhood Forum 2003), to support practitioners as well as gain political attention.

There has also been a plethora of policies and initiatives developed to support families in achieving economic well-being by providing affordable and accessible childcare. References to play in relation to 'quality provision' have become increasingly visible in these policies and initiatives. However, adjectives such as 'structured', 'adult-directed', 'purposeful', 'child-initiated' and 'planned' have also been linked to play. In addition, phrases such as 'self-directed activity' or 'active/experiential learning' are used to describe the play experiences of children when these are freely chosen. This has resulted in a lack of clarity in relation to the meanings and therefore conceptualisations of good practice in relation to play.

What then have been the government's legislation, documentation and initiatives over recent years, and to what extent do they make explicit reference to play? The following provides a brief history of the major documents.

1994: Early Years Task Force

This included representatives from government departments including Treasury, Health, Employment and Education, academics and practitioners who created a statement of intent containing eight principles. The first of these related to the needs of young children and parents and made a commitment to providing learning, play, socialisation and care for children and adults. Central to this was the recognition that ethnic and cultural diversity should be valued and appropriately responded to. It was the principles of this task force that provided the foundation on which later early years policy was built. These principles reflected the priorities of the day, informed by research, scholarship and practice.

In 1996 the government introduced the voucher scheme for nursery education for 4 year olds. This was the first state funding for a universal early years service. While the intention was to provide an increase in the quantity of provision, it was not long before the issue of quality within settings arose again.

1996: Desirable Outcomes for Children's Learning on Entering Compulsory Education

This was a very concise document in which the term 'play' was only used twice in the section discussing the six outcomes, and once as a 'medium for learning' (page 6) in the section describing 'Common features of good practice'.

The desirable outcomes were linked to the following areas:

- personal and social development
- language and literacy
- mathematics
- knowledge and understanding of the world
- creative development
- physical development.

Concern was expressed on the publication of this document regarding its appropriateness for young children due to the emphasis placed on 'outcomes' or products rather than processes. The content was also perceived by some as setting unrealistic expectations of young children. Alexander and others (1999) describes the statements as requiring children to be 'prenaturally mature'.

1998: National Childcare Strategy

This was part of the government's anti-poverty strategy to expand *good quality* childcare provision to enable parents to return to work. It represented considerable growth in childcare provision but brought with it concerns that it would discourage parents from staying at home with young babies. To offset this, paid maternity leave was increased to 26 weeks, two weeks paternity leave was later introduced, and parents with children under six could request flexible working from their employers (Pugh 2005).

1999: Early Learning Goals

These consist of six areas of learning similar to those documented in the *Desirable Outcomes*. They are:

- personal, social and emotional development
- communication, language and literacy
- mathematical development
- knowledge and understanding of the world
- creative development
- physical development.

Although similar in name to the *Desirable Outcomes for Children's Learning*, the addition of 'emotional' development to the first goal and 'communication' to the second, as well as changing 'mathematics' to 'mathematical development' appeared to reflect a greater understanding of, and emphasis on, child development.

2000: Introduction of the Foundation Stage (3–5 years)

The Early Years Curriculum Group (2002) saw the introduction of the Foundation Stage as problematic because it connected early experience and learning to better achievement later. There was also concern regarding the emphasis on inspections of literacy and numeracy and the top-down pressure of Year 2 standard assessment tests (SATs) which set inappropriate expectations for young children.

Although the intention was that this document would encourage practitioners in reception classes to provide a more holistic experience such as that offered in nursery practice, Adams and others (2004) discovered that reception class pedagogy had moved inappropriately towards that of Key Stage 1.

2000: Curriculum Guidance for the Foundation Stage

This document emphasises that it is not a curriculum in itself but contains guidance regarding outcomes *towards which* children in the Foundation Stage (children aged 3–5 years) should be working. One of the principles for early years education is documented as: 'there should be opportunities for children to engage in activities planned by adults and also those that they plan or initiate themselves. Children do not make a distinction between "play" and "work" and neither should practitioners' (Qualifications and Curriculum Authority 2000: 11).

The curriculum guidance devotes one page specifically to 'play' with an emphasis on 'well-planned' play. This section highlights the role of the adult in play and the potential benefits to children of play. While the emphasis on play in the document was welcomed by many, there was also concern that the term 'well-planned' was not defined, and therefore much depends on the pedagogy and value base of individual practitioners as to how this is worked out in practice. In contrast, much less emphasis is given in the document to 'free' or 'spontaneous' play.

As mentioned earlier, Adams and others (2004) discovered in their evaluation of reception classes that the curriculum guidance *was* being viewed by educators as the curriculum.

2001: National Standards for Daycare and Childminding

These consisted of 14 standards ranging from those concerned with a suitable person to work in daycare to safety, health, child protection and documentation. Standard 3 was entitled *Care, Learning and Play*. In this the role of the practitioner was described as one that meets children's emotional, physical, social and intellectual capabilities.

In the guidance to the national standards it stated that this is achieved through 'sensitive and appropriate interactions that promote children's self-esteem'. The guidance continued to describe the role of the adult as one in which children are enabled to *make choices* that are monitored regularly to provide information to respond to individual needs. In the section entitled 'Points to consider', 'building relationships and developing self-esteem' and 'learning and play opportunities' feature. In the latter sub-section, practitioners were guided to provide a wide range of planned and free play opportunities both inside and outside, and through visits and outings. In addition, providers were informed that inspectors made judgements regarding the extent to which children were 'making decisions about their play and their learning as they choose from a range of activities'.

2003: Birth to Three Matters framework

Following work sharply focused on children in the years immediately prior to statutory schooling, there was concern that the needs of babies and toddlers were being neglected. From projects developed with these very young children, the Birth to Three Matters framework was produced to support practitioners working with them.

Birth to Three Matters consists of four 'aspects' entitled:

- A Strong Child
- A Skilful Communicator
- A Competent Learner
- A Healthy Child.

Each aspect is broken down into a number of constituent parts called components.

The booklet contained in the Birth to Three Matters toolkit describes the intention of the framework: to provide 'support, guidance and challenge for all those with responsibility for the care and education of babies from birth to three years' (Sure Start 2003: 4). The toolkit contains resources to support practitioners, including laminated cards that contain a section relating to 'play and practical support'. Adults are also given guidance as to what they can do to support young children. For example, in the aspect, A Skilful Communicator, they are encouraged to participate in listening and responding by making playful responses. In other aspects they are to observe and join in play. Adults are expected to plan play and provide play situations in order that children can experience role, pretend and symbolic play.

As part of the implementation of the Childcare Act 2006, the Early Years Foundation Stage draws together Birth to Three Matters, the Foundation Stage and the National Standards for Daycare and Childminding.

2003: Every Child Matters

This is one of the most significant initiatives for children in recent years. It is a national framework created to promote local changes. It reflects a determination to increase quality, accessibility and coherence of services and to enable children to fulfil their potential. Local leaders are required to work in partnership with local communities. Every Child Matters has five outcomes, which are regarded as being the key to well-being in childhood and later life:

- *Be healthy* – includes physical, mental, emotional and sexual dimensions and promotes healthy lifestyles.
- *Stay safe* – promotes security, stability, being cared for as well as raising awareness of maltreatment, accidental injury and death, bullying, discrimination, crime and anti-social behaviour.
- *Enjoy and achieve* – academic achievement, personal and social development, play and recreation are supported.
- *Make a positive contribution* – through decision making, positive relationships, self-confidence and enterprising behaviour.
- *Achieve economic well-being* – becoming ready for employment.

This heralds a radical change to children's services through integration of services with shared responsibility, early specialised help where necessary, provision of services around the child and family, dedicated leadership, shared responsibility and the commitment to listening to children, young people and their families.

2004: The Children Act

This Act reflects a determination to increase quality, accessibility and coherence of services. In the Act the five Every Child Matters outcomes were given legal force. It also established a Children's Commissioner to represent the views and interests of families and young people. In order to meet the requirements laid down in the Act, cooperation between agencies is required. A duty is placed on local authorities to safeguard children, appoint a Director of Children's Services, create an integrated inspection framework for foster care and private fostering and the education of children in care. Amendments to the Act define the term 'young child' as one who is between birth and the first September following the fifth birthday. Early years provision is understood similarly as provision for young children within that timeframe.

2004: The Five-Year Strategy for Children and Learners and the Ten-Year Strategy for Childcare

These focus on integrated services, better access for parents to education and childcare, and more choice for parents. The key principles of the Ten-Year Strategy have been enshrined in law in the Childcare Act 2006.

2004: The National Service Framework

This is a 10-year plan to change thinking about children's health. The aim is to look at the child and not just illness, and 12 standards are identified to raise quality and to move to a more preventative approach to children's health.

2006: The Childcare Act

This Act redefines childcare. It speaks of 'high quality childcare' for children under five and their families. The views of parents are to be heard and there are to be improved outcomes for all children under five through integrated and accessible services. The Early Years Foundation Stage (from birth to age five) which is to be introduced in September 2008 will draw together the present Birth to Three Matters framework, the Foundation Stage, and the National Standards for Daycare and Childminding, with the aim of ensuring delivery and integration of education and care for children from birth to age five. In order to ensure a suitably qualified workforce, the government has created a Transformation Fund of £250 million to invest in this purpose. This will support the growth of graduate level early years professionals (EYPs). The national standards for the EYP include Standard 11, a sub-section of Effective Practice, which relates to children's play by stating that the EYP should be able to: 'Plan and provide safe and appropriate child-led and adult-initiated experiences, activities and play opportunities in indoor, outdoor and out-of-setting contexts, which enable children to develop and learn' (Children's Workforce Development Council 2006: 9).

The government has recently completed a period of consultation regarding the introduction of the Early Years Foundation Stage. The lengthy consultation document made explicit that play is to be fostered in young children. However, a close reading of the document reveals that more emphasis is placed on 'purposeful' and 'planned' play than on children's 'free' play. Whilst many early childhood practitioners understand this to mean that adults structure and plan the environments for play, rather than the play itself, this is not made explicit and may not be understood in this way by all practitioners.

It is apparent from these initiatives, that play is increasingly being recognised as important in the experience of young children, but there is still a lack of clarity regarding its nature and potential benefits.

The above policies have led to a change in the form and content of provision for children and their families. Over the past decade there have been a number of initiatives introduced, as outlined in the following sub-sections.

1997–2006: Early Excellence Centres

These were designed to foster the integration of care and education of young children. Objectives were developed in relation to local needs. At present, funding has been extended until spring

2008. Findings from the EPPE project mentioned earlier noted that combined centres produce the best outcomes in relation to higher attainment of children at the start of primary school.

1999–2006: Sure Start programmes

These emphasise family support and integrated services for families with young children to tackle child poverty and social inequalities, primarily through health services and community development. Poor health means that children are unlikely to achieve their potential at school. This provision has brought core services together. Programmes are locally administered and have parents on their management boards.

1999: Sure Start Second Wave Objectives and Targets

This wave included four targets, of which the second was 'Improving the ability to learn'. All children in Sure Start areas should be able to access good quality play and early learning opportunities to promote the *Early Learning Goals*.

2000–2006: The Neighbourhood Nursery Initiative

This provided new provision in disadvantaged areas in order to reduce child poverty and provide high quality childcare and early learning. Evaluations of this provision focus on the use of centres, the hours the provision is accessible and the range of services provided, rather than the impact on children and families.

2002–present: Children's Centres

The government has committed itself to providing 2,500 Children's Centres by 2008 and 3,100 by 2010. This programme is to be developed in two phases: phase 1 in the 20 per cent most disadvantaged wards and phase 2 in the next 30 per cent most disadvantaged wards. Children's development is intended as being at the heart of these. There is a commitment to ensuring that quality of staff, environment, and play opportunities are all high.

As discussed earlier, there is currently a major workforce restructuring taking place. The introduction of the EYP is part of this. The government anticipates that by 2010 there will be an EYP in all Children's Centres offering childcare, and in full daycare settings by 2015. This is a new role for those who meet the required standards and fulfil the requirements.

Play is enjoying a renaissance at present. The programmes mentioned above suggest that play is positively regarded in the lives of young children and an integral element of high quality provision. Large-scale projects such as the Effective Provision of Preschool Education Project (Sylva and others 2004) funded by the government, and the Study of Pedagogical Effectiveness in Early Learning (Moyles and others 2002) both talk of the importance of play in high quality provision. Generally, however, 'play' is an ill-defined and all-encompassing term that requires further examination.

In cultures such as our own, play is often not taken seriously. Bruce (2005) argues, however, that free-flow play is at the centre of humanity across all parts of the world and within ancient civilisations. She places play where she considers it belongs, at the centre of humanity, for it is crucial for individuals, communities and cultures. Fagen (1981) suggests that, because across all cultures children play without encouragement, there must be some sort of play instinct.

Hughes (2001), from an evolutionary play perspective, observes that play is universal among mammals. He interprets its complexity as an indicator of its evolutionary development from the genesis of time to the contemporary period. Evolutionary psychology is a relatively new field of study, which has developed from the synergy of cognitive psychology and evolutionary biology. It espouses the view that the design of the mind evolves as a result of natural selection. As it adapts for the purposes of survival the mind evolves new mental structures, develops flexibility and creates new combinations of thought and action in play. From this perspective, play is therefore an inherently powerful biological force.

Garvey (1991) believes that play is humanity's biological heritage, which has a culture-creating capacity. She understands play as being systematic and rule-governed and in which, if observed closely, regular patterns can be discerned.

Garvey (1991: 4, 5) goes on to describe the features of play as:

- pleasure and enjoyment – it is valued by the player
- intrinsically motivated and without extrinsic goals – play can be inherently unproductive
- spontaneous and freely chosen
- active engagement by the player
- *systematically* related to what is not play – that is, creativity, problem solving, language learning and the development of social roles.

These features of play are common threads throughout play literature.

Opie (1993) noted the paradox and advantage of play in that it is both serious and inconsequential: 'A game is a microcosm, more powerful and important than any individual player: yet when it is finished it is finished, and nothing depends on the outcome' (Opie 1993: 15). From this perspective, outcomes are not considered to be the child's focus when playing. However, deep learning does take place during play.

Bruce (2001) outlines 12 important features of play that describe in more detail how children behave, and what they are doing in play. These features are:

- In their play, children use the first-hand experiences that they have in life.
- Children make up the rules as they play, and so keep control of their play.
- Children make play props.
- Children choose to play. They cannot be made to play.
- Children rehearse the future in their role-play.
- Children pretend when they play.
- Children play alone sometimes.
- Children and adults play together, in parallel, associatively, or cooperatively in pairs or groups.
- Each player has a personal agenda, although they may not be aware of this.

- Children playing will be deeply involved and difficult to distract from their deep learning. Children at play wallow in their learning.
- Children try out their most recent learning, skills and competencies when they play. They seem to celebrate what they know.
- Children at play coordinate their ideas, feelings and make sense of their relationships with their family, friends and culture.

There is therefore some agreement between these writers that play is intrinsically motivated and powerful both in the affective and cognitive domains, both in the immediate and the long term.

The affective and cognitive dimensions of play are closely related and interlinked. Therefore the emotional contexts in which children grow up influence their later emotional dispositions, development of relationships, and the extent to which they physically explore the world. Crucial to this are secure attachments to carers in the early years of life (Bowlby 1969; Rutter 1972; Schaffer 1971). When children have a strong, secure relationship with their immediate carers then play exchanges between the two develop spontaneously For example peek-a-boo games foster both a positive sense of self in the child and stimulate cognitive development. Because the child is given time and attention the child learns that he or she has worth. However, during the play the child can also test out consistent behaviour, predict reactions and explore cause and effect. Initially the adult initiates the game, but as the child grows they can take the initiative. Hughes (2001) describes such play as the actions of a lone child carrying out evolutionary behaviour by seeking to establish links with other humans, species and systems, following the pattern set out in evolution. Brown (2003) from the same perspective describes (on page 11) the play between child and carer as an act that incorporates the other into one's own 'realm of understanding'. When young children are secure with their carers then they tend to be more gregarious and engage in complex play with other children.

It is this secure relationship that is fundamental to the child's developing autonomy and self-confidence. By 12 months, securely attached children are more likely to explore the world independently than insecurely attached children. This is important because physical exploration of the world through the senses is the predominant way in which children learn in the first two years of life. This is a stage that Piaget (1971) calls the sensori-motor stage. During this, children acquire control over their movements and repeat and vary these. Although Piaget's theory of *stages* is challenged today as being too rigid and not taking account of the unpredictable nature of learning, the fact that children learn through first-hand exploration is generally accepted.

Play and exploration

The seminal work of Hutt and others (1989) was instrumental in drawing our attention to the many types of play that children engage in, including the physical exploration of materials. The authors draw them together in a taxonomy under three main headings: 'epistemic', 'ludic' and 'games with rules'. Their research was a study of over 1,000 children in more than 50 preschool establishments in two areas. Time-sampled observations, recordings and questionnaires to staff were used to gain insights into the children's play. As a result of their findings the authors made a distinction between play and exploration. In epistemic play children were exploring the properties of materials through physical manipulation. They were finding out what the materials could do. This exploration requires deep concentration during which the child learns all there is to know about the objects. Features of their engagement during this play were:

- the acquisition of information – things that are soft or hard, smooth or textured, sour or sweet
- manipulation, inspection and investigation
- activities designed to bring change to material
- effort, attention and purposeful activities that have objectives and goals.

Once this knowledge has been obtained, it is then incorporated into play activity.

In contrast, ludic play (which is imaginative and fantasy play) involved self-amusement, a relaxed state, imposition of constraints by the child, imaginative or pretend play, repetition (sometimes with new features) and exaggeration. Through this, children find out what they can do with the materials.

Almost all the teachers in Hutt and others' (1989) research sample believed that 'fantasy play' was important both in terms of the child's emotional needs and as an aid to linguistic and cognitive development. Much of the children's fantasy play was very simple, with simple objects. However quite complex themes could develop when the props were more flexible. When children got to know one another and were relaxed, fantasy play increased. The authors concluded that such play therefore only occurs in positive affective states. In this research the amount of fantasy play did not correlate with IQ, social class or personality. However, of the four measures of linguistic complexity, three were significantly greater in play than in normal discourse. Fantasy play gave insights into a child's mood, past experiences and hidden talents.

In their taxonomy, Hutt and others (1989) subdivide 'games with rules' into four categories: cooperative, games of chance, games of skill and competitive games. They suggest that games with rules lie somewhere between epistemic and ludic play. One feature of games with rules is that they have their own rituals and conventions, and may be highly socially constrained. It is the content of a game say Hutt and colleagues that determines whether or not it is play. In the same way that the same activity can be work for one person and play for another, for example for a child a game of football may be play, but for a professional footballer it may be perceived as work, so it is in games with rules.

Hutt and others (1989), contrary to the work of other theorists, found that children by the age of five do make a distinction between work and play. This distinction emanates from the degree of constraint that they experience. If children feel constraints placed on what they do, and how and when they do it, they then describe the activity as work. Play was a matter of 'feeling free'. The authors conclude that free play is important in psychological development, but that this should be balanced with epistemic activity.

Goldschmied and Jackson (1994) have developed an approach to working with babies and toddlers that has fundamental similarities to Hutt and others' (1989) epistemic play. This approach includes the 'treasure basket' for children aged 6–9 months and 'heuristic play' for children from 12–20 months. Although Goldschmied and Jackson suggest that the evidence for play enhancing learning in the areas of language development, problem solving, creativity and social adjustment is inconclusive, they subscribe to the view that play is important. Their book is written for practitioners, particularly in the daycare or childminding context, to 'encourage complex, concentrated play in preference to aimless flitting from one thing to another' (page 9). Since their book was published, much has been written about play. The work of Athey (1990) for instance has given insights that reinterpret what Goldschmied and Jackson describe as the 'flitting' behaviours of children as deeply focused cognitive activity. This study is discussed later.

Goldschmied and Jackson advocate the use of a 'treasure basket' (a basket full of natural materials such as pine cones, shells and household objects) for the child between 6 and 9 months. Children are observed to spend long periods of time engaged in exploring the materials through the senses. As they do so they make choices, show preferences, make decisions, express pleasure and develop hand—eye coordination as they lift, throw and draw materials to their mouths. This experience fosters the child's natural curiosity. The adult acts as an 'emotional anchor' and fosters confidence and concentration without actively participating. The interactions of the child can provide adults with invaluable opportunities to make observations through which they can increase their understanding of, and sensitivity to, young children.

At 12–20 months when children become mobile, they are introduced to heuristic play. The word 'heuristic' is from the Greek word *eurisko*, which means 'serves to discover or reach understanding of' (Goldschmied and Jackson 1994: 119). It is spontaneous, exploratory activity. During heuristic play periods, groups of children are provided with bags of different objects and materials such as balls, cylinders, tins, ribbons and chains, which they then use as they wish. These open-ended materials are interesting, promote challenge and children can combine materials as they choose, for example putting chains through tubes or cones on top of bottles or tins. Children can discover through free play understanding of concepts such as movement, shape, space, mass, length, weight, one-to-one correspondence and seriation as they select, compare and combine objects. Goldschmied and Jackson have observed children in different countries and conclude that in heuristic play:

- children work with purpose and concentration
- physical energy and manipulation are observed
- constant practice and gains in competence occur
- there is no right or wrong use of materials so no predetermined outcome is expected
- conflict with peers is reduced when a wide range of materials are available (although we must note that this in turn may rob the child of the opportunity to share and negotiate even at a most basic level)
- cooperation develops as a natural outcome of co-focus
- there is an internal logic.

Constant availability of this type of play leads to play becoming more varied and complex over time. As children help to clear away the materials and store them in bags they learn about routines, share responsibility, develop a sense of time and extend their vocabulary by naming the objects. Siraj-Blatchford and Siraj-Blatchford (2002) highlight the fact that in experimental play such as this, children begin to categorise objects, which comes before the development of more complex knowledge and understanding in mathematics and science.

There is a link between exploration of objects and materials and the growth of the brain. Brierley (1994) suggests that physical exploration of this sort is vital in building in the brain a model or understanding of the world: 'Exploration is essential if we are to build up in the brain a representation or "model" which is useful for the accurate interpretation of the world … building up knowledge of the world through our senses and by trial and error is the basis of all later intellectual activity' (Brierley 1994: 75 and 76).

Early experience and brain development

Research into brain development illustrates the way in which the experiences that children have in their early years impact not only on the biological structure of the brain but also the child's ability to learn. Immediately after birth there is an increase in the growth of nerves and neural pathways in the brain as well as the connections between these. This is particularly so from 2 years to early adolescence. Up to the age of five there is a major increase in the growth of cells and synapses. Sutton-Smith (1997) reminds us that the infant's brain undergoes major physical and chemical changes as it responds to the environment, creating plasticity or flexibility. If the child experiences an impoverished environment and the neural pathways are not used, then a radical pruning takes place (Griffiths, J 2003). Therefore part of the function of play is to bring about the achievement of the brain's potential. Conversely lack of stimulus may result in the loss of some of these connections.

During the years of swift brain growth a child's eyes, ears and sense of touch in particular are absorbing experiences of all kinds through the types of exploration described above. The *quality* of these experiences is vital for complex brain development as they affect how nerves develop, their density and the interconnections made between them (Family and Work Institute 1996). John Griffiths (2003) reminds us, however, that to date there is no evidence that the density of these connections, or brain size, is proof of greater intellect.

The development and interconnections of the brain's neural pathways are vital for passing messages speedily to, and from, different parts of the body in order to get things done. These nerves, however, cannot function effectively until they are covered with a coating of myelin to ensure that no information is lost, and that the message travels directly to the intended receptor. It is interesting to note that the brain is programmed to give primacy to the development of visual competence, which in turn facilitates epistemic and exploratory play experiences that are crucial to further development of the nervous system. The nerve fibres that carry information from the eyes and the organs of touch are myelinated before the areas that control movement, thus enabling the brain to see where objects are, providing the sensation of touch in order to facilitate control of simple movements: 'The activity of the motor system is initiated and controlled through its sensory connections. During the early years children explore constantly and their activities develop gross and fine motor control' (Brierley 1994: 26).

Practice speeds ups and automates these responses until they become automated. Practice and repetition in children's play, rather than being a sign of purposeless activity, are central in building the child's brain and creating rapid responses within the central nervous system. Brown (2003) asserts that play is a context spontaneously created by, and for, experience. In addition Isenberg and Quisenberry (2002) emphasise that play is a way of scaffolding or supporting development through the development of neural structures. Through it children are building up their understanding of the world, which is consolidated and adapted as further experiences either consolidate or contradict previous learning.

The development of memory, and social and emotional functioning, are higher functions of the brain. This aspect of brain development is not complete until a child is 5 or 6 years of age. Memory traces are made in the brain of 'significant' experiences. These memories need constant practice and repetition. Garvey (1991) regards this repetition and practice as central to the child's play.

Brierley goes on to warn that if children are introduced inappropriately to the formal practice of skills to the detriment of time to explore and investigate the world at a motor level, then their curiosity, motivation and creativity may be impaired: 'The developing motor intelligence should not be blunted by too early an introduction to specific skills and techniques or over-practising skills which at this stage impair imagination and the readiness to explore' (Brierley 1994: 26).

Although John Griffiths (2003) agrees that 'too formal too soon' can create long-term problems, he suggests that comparative studies show that later formal skill development, when cognitive systems are in place to cope with them, does no harm.

Brierley (1994) also reminds us that the child does not learn from experience alone but that the child learns, and the brain develops, from the common experiences of childhood – including play. However, he believes that it is motivation and autonomy that promote intelligent activity and are deeply influential: 'A child does not learn from a passive kaleidoscope of experiences but from the outcomes of actions that he or she has initiated' (Brierley 1994: 75).

More recently, research on brain development has given cause for caution, particularly in relation to optimum periods for learning. John Griffiths (2003) reminds us that the research into critical periods, where irreversible damage is perceived to occur if an organism misses one or several critical periods, often investigates only extreme situations. The majority of organisms do develop in impoverished environments. Due to brain plasticity (or flexibility), intervention at any point can make a difference to children's development if the problems are not catastrophically severe. The right kind of intervention is necessary, but clearly prevention through activity and experience is a better option.

Play and the emotional worlds of young children

Psychoanalysts regard the emotions as driving forces in behaviour. Freud (Sigmund and Anna), Erikson and Isaacs regard play both as a means of expressing emotions that are in the conscious, and as a process by which children come to terms with difficult situations and painful emotions, such as the birth of a new baby or a visit to the dentist or hospital, that are stored in the pre or subconscious. Through play, children explore and express their emotions. They overcome fear and anxiety through enacting real scenarios in their role and socio-dramatic play. Herron and Sutton-Smith (1971: 113) remind us that play can 'mitigate the traumatic effect of a recent experience'. By facing these challenges at a distance the child can address uncomfortable issues, and therefore the impact of the experience is lessened. As Erikson (1950) so eruditely states: 'Solitary play remains an indispensable harbour for the overhauling of shattered emotions after periods of rough going in the social seas' (Erikson 1950: 194).

Through play, children reveal their inner feelings. Therefore play is a form of catharsis and a way of gaining emotional balance and maintaining healthy mental well-being. It fosters 'resilience to stressful life events' (Street 2002: 1).

The Mental Health Foundation (1999) highlights the importance of children being 'emotionally literate' by being able to play, take risks, use their initiative, make friends and deal with conflict. Such play may reduce the risk of some children having mental health problems in later life. Busby (1994), observing children with emotional problems in a playgroup, noted that they chose either to play alone or seek out an adult. Although withdrawal from the group may be an instinctive immediate response to dissipate stress, in the long term the author considers that this could hinder children's social development.

Goleman (1996) suggests that emotions are the main force in all human behaviour. He has shown that 'emotional intelligence', or the ability to handle feelings and emotions successfully, may be more significant than IQ in terms of a child's long-term attainment.

> School success is not predicted by a child's fund of facts, or by a precocious ability to read so much as by emotional and social measures; being self assured and interested; knowing what kind of behaviour is expected and how to rein in impulse to misbehave; being able to wait; to follow directions and to turn to adults and peers for help; expressing needs whilst getting along with other children. (Goleman 1996: 193)

Hohmann and Weikart (1995), promoters of the High/Scope curriculum approach that supports children in decision making, autonomy and self-efficacy, describe the self-assurance that comes from healthy emotional development as the 'core of inner pride' that grows as a result of opportunities for autonomous behaviour, empowering children to take responsibility and become risk-takers. This is positive self-esteem.

When children play out their emotional concerns, adults may not always understand either their pressing nature, or have a repertoire of responses to deal with them appropriately. Holland (2003) and Rich (2003) both write about war, weapons and superhero play in early years settings. While acknowledging the concerns of adults in this respect, they question zero tolerance of gun play when children access such images almost daily through the media. For some children, the course of their daily lives, or their histories, have brought them into much closer contact with war, weapons, death and destruction.

Rich (2003) and Holland (2003) postulate that it is predominantly boys who are interested in this type of play. They suggest that it is frequently met with 'corrective and punitive' responses from adults. They believe that adults should look beyond the external behaviour to the themes that lie below the surface. In gun play children may be visiting, at a safe distance, issues of life and death or re-enacting power and powerlessness roles, as well as developing their gross motor skills. They are developing their skills as players – their cognitive capacity and commitment to learning. Rich (2003) emphasises that such play should be supported by policies that value children's cultural heritage. When adults model toleration then children learn to tolerate others, negotiate, listen, empathise, work and function, think through, and consider the effects of possible actions. These are essential life skills and future world skills. Through gun play, children can play out potential solutions and story line options.

Rich observes that children's play reflects:

- what they have experienced
- what they are interested in
- what they know about (to the limits of their knowledge)
- what they want to know more about
- what they want to understand
- what they are anxious, concerned or worried about
- what they feel
- their many possible future roles.

Through play, children express their feelings. It is a form of therapy. The role of the adult is to develop an understanding of the child's emotional state and be aware that this can influence other aspects of the child's world. As Rich and Holland comment, observation of children's play may indicate a disturbance, but identifying the underlying cause is more difficult. Some children may not possess the vocabulary of emotions to help them articulate their situation, or indeed they may not want to, for children learn to disguise and suppress painful emotions. The skilled adult must foster a relationship in which the child feels secure, being sensitive and respectful of the child's right to share or withhold information and being empathetic when the opportunity manifests itself.

The work of Paley (1988) is also of particular interest here, because her books reveal the deeply reflective accounts of a kindergarten teacher who is committed to developing her understanding of the children in her care. In her book, *Bad Guys Don't Have Birthdays*, she records the story of Frederick who has recently had a baby brother.

Frederick's silence on the event concerns his teacher, particularly when her attempts to help him express his feelings fall on stony ground. Frederick experiences sadness because of the loss of his position in the family and is anxious and fearful. Paley observes him repeatedly adopting the role of the baby in his play to the extent that it annoys his peers.

Paley's wider writings reveal that children in their imaginative play are struggling with deep philosophical issues such as birth and death, good and evil, and power and powerlessness. They are examining the power of rules and searching for ways of neutralising evil: 'The children were actors on a moving stage, carrying on philosophical debates while borrowing fragments of floating dialogue, themes from fairy tales and television, cartoons combined with social commentary and private fantasy to form a tangible script that was not random and erratic' (Paley 1988: 16).

Frost (2005) reminds us of the therapeutic benefits of play for children who are in, or have come from, areas where natural disasters occur, such as the effects of the recent tsunami, Hurricane Katrina, disease in Africa and genocide disasters. His experiences have given him an insight into these disasters and the effects that they have on children's physical and emotional health. As a play therapist he advocates the therapeutic powers of spontaneous play and 'meaningful work'. He believes that 'skilled and charitable adults can sustain and heal children to help bring them joy'. He cites the work of Grossfield (1997) and Raymond and Raymond (2000), who found that children attempt to express themselves through play, work and the creative arts even in the most bizarre and brutal conditions. During tragic situations, human beings show great energy and the ability to adapt to present and future needs. They observe that the drive to play is so strong that even in the holocaust children were recorded as acting out fairy tales in the cemetery.

Frost believes that play and the creative arts help children cope with fear and trauma by providing a medium for self-expression. By these means children can express the thoughts and concerns for which they have no words. They release feelings and frustrations and thus maintain mental well-being. In psychoanalytical terms, through play children express emotions that relate to situations that they have no control over. This helps to develop mastery over stressful situations.

Frost details the role of the adult in this context as giving children hope and dignity, providing close emotional support and accepting the reality that children are fearful, confused and upset. Children need to understand that their emotions are natural. As in any bereavement, it is important to talk about the tragedy in simple language without speculation or embellishment, and respect local customs, religious beliefs and belief systems. It is important for the child to have contact with familiar people. They should participate in make-believe play, have access to natural areas such as gardens and woodlands, and be encouraged to write stories, poems and plays.

Hughes (2001) and Brown (2003) from an evolutionary playwork perspective give credence to the power of the environment, not only to impact on children's brain development and their emotional functioning, but also to bring about a connection with their evolutionary roots through contact with natural elements such as fire, earth, air and water, and other species and systems. They warn that cutting off children from the natural world will cause a disconnection from their evolutionary past and may make children ill. Connections with the earth are crucial to the child's identity, which, in the case of trauma as described above, may need to be re-established.

The construction of identity and relationships in play

Literature dealing with children's social development is generally well documented. Reddy and Trevarthen (2004) believe that children have an innate engagement in the world as is evidenced in their gestures and 'pre-speech'. Trevarthen (2005) identifies 'intersubjectivity' (now called sympathy) as an important feature in developing relationships with babies. This is the capacity of two or more people to perceive subjectivity in others' behaviour and for each to adapt. Through early playful relationships, babies and toddlers are constructing views of themselves as individuals; that they are interesting, worthy of attention and can be partners in exchanges with those around them. Goldschmied and Jackson (1994) describe the child as using the mother's body as her first toy, when she grasps her caregiver's fingers, handles her breast and grabs at her hair, jewellery or spectacles.

Play is a primary means by which peers identify with one another, yet at the same time recognise differences. It is the primary medium for the creation of social networks, learning what the norms are in these and developing a sense of self. Bruner (1996) believes that the sense of self and awareness of others as individual 'selves' is fundamental to the education system: 'A system of education must help those growing up in a culture find an identity within that culture. Without it, they stumble in their effort after meaning' (Bruner 1996: 42).

Through role-play, children learn about themselves and others, and develop empathy. Socio-dramatic play (in a group) helps children to see things from the point of view of others. They learn the social skills of sharing, turn-taking and negotiation. Dunn (1983) states that peer relationships are characterised by reciprocity and that high levels of social play and management of conflicts are central to reciprocal relationships. In addition, the potential for the development of vocabulary and language skills is limitless.

Langsted (1994) reminds us that children play, practise and learn at the same time. The game itself and social relationships are the most important things, skills and competencies are by-products. Through play and peer relations, children develop strategies for dealing with the outside world.

Broadhead (2001), in the second phase of her work in reception settings, investigated the sociability and cooperation play of four and five year olds. Her research was carried out in schools with high levels of poverty and unemployment. She sought to describe the language and actions that children use when they are being sociable and cooperative with peers. During data collection, children were observed to have long periods of play without adult involvement. Thirty-seven play periods were observed ranging from 4 to 47 minutes in duration. The average length of a play bout was 24 minutes.

Broadhead developed a social play continuum based on the work of Parten (1933). In this, play moves along the continuum from associative play (in which children play alongside each other without interaction) to social, highly social and then cooperative play. During associative play there is no, or very little, discourse. The child looks, watches and imitates. A feature of social play is the disposition of children to leave and join play at frequent intervals. As a consequence, there is little development of ideas, for the child may just receive an object, instruction, request, or comment on the action. In contrast, in high social play the group is relatively stable. Suggestions emerge that briefly extend the original play ideas; adult intervention is sometimes sought to resolve altercations; offering and accepting objects is an explicit act and comments on actions lead to discourse; discourse leads to eye contact, laughter, play and noise. During cooperative play the play remains in one location until the completion of goals. There is imaginative use of materials and ideas, absence of play noises, absorption in the task, altercations are resolved within the play as a problem-solving activity, and adult intervention is not sought until the end. Children exchange smiles and explanations, interaction extends play, problems are identified and solved, and goal orientation is evident.

Broadhead observed that as children's play progressed it became more cognitively and socially demanding. Children were observed to engage in 'self-tutoring' when talking to themselves. This self-talk increasingly served problem solving and planning as the child's activities grew more complex. This reflects Vygotsky's perspective that if talk is a transitional stage from vocal to inner speech, it is associated with mental functions (Vygotsky 1962).

As children's play moved towards cooperation on Broadhead's continuum, children functioned more independently and cooperatively with increasing reciprocity. In social play, interactions were brief. Cooperative play sustained problem solving and revealed deep intellectual commitment. Play became more interactive, more challenging and potentially more satisfying when there were opportunities to build sequences of reciprocal action. Broadhead refers to the interrelationship between the affective and cognitive dimensions of play: 'Social and cooperative interactions provide emotional outlets and individual satisfaction along with intellectual challenge, hence their inherent attraction to children' (Broadhead 2001: 33).

This echoes Hutt and others' (1989) thesis that fantasy play increases when children get to know one another and are relaxed. The authors also concluded that such play therefore only occurs in positive affective states.

Broadhead asserts that through free play the child is learning the skills that are needed to sustain sociable and cooperative intent in a problem-solving and intellectually challenging context. Sociability and cooperation are skilful, cognitively informed behaviours that need practice to aid development. Without encouragement to explore their world through play, children are likely to develop difficulties in forming healthy relationships.

It would be erroneous to assert that play is always a happy process for the child, because it can provoke conflict and unhappiness as well as give pleasure (Vygotsky 1962). In play children have the opportunity to solve their own conflicts (Langsted 1994). The High/Scope curriculum offers a problem-solving approach to social conflict (Hohmann and Weikart 1995). This process encourages adults to avoid prematurely intervening in the situation so that children have the opportunity to resolve their own conflicts. The approach involves adults in working through an explicit process in which they support children in expressing their feelings, and negotiating and seeking their own solutions to their problems. The process has six steps:

1. Approach calmly
2. Acknowledge feelings
3. Gather information
4. Restate the problem

5. Ask for solutions and choose one together
6. Be prepared to give follow up and support.

The High/Scope approach, based on the work of Piaget, has been implemented for more than 40 years. The curriculum is composed of a daily routine that balances child-initiated and adult-initiated activities. The 'plan – do – review' aspect, which is unique to High/Scope, provides children with the opportunity to choose and plan their play, carry out their intentions, and then reflect and review their actions. After children plan their play they *all* engage in free play, therefore the adult is available to observe or to support them in their interests. Berry and Sylva (1987) report that, over time, children's plans increase in complexity from 'vague' to 'routine' to 'detailed'. In an evaluation of the implementation of the curriculum in four preschool settings across England, staff reported that as a result of the new approach there was an improvement in children's language development, an increase in their concentration skills and more pro-social behaviour (Santer 2000).

A longitudinal study carried out in the United States by the High/Scope Research Foundation drew attention to the long-term social benefits of the High/Scope curriculum in which a central element is child-initiated play that is also planned. The research compared 123 African-American children randomly assigned to either an experimental group, which experienced preschool provision, or a control group with no preschool experience. The children were part of the lowest income group within the area and had IQs of below 85. The principal measurement used at the beginning of the study was intellectual ability. The study showed that on entry to school the experimental group had an increased IQ compared with the control group. They were also considered less aggressive, less disruptive and more obedient. Data over time showed that the initial IQ gains washed out (this is typical of many cognitive programmes) but that there were significant social benefits both to the individual and society over time. By age 19 the children who had attended pre-school provision were more likely to:

- become high school graduates
- continue in college or job training
- be in employment
- financially support themselves and their spouses
- report satisfaction with their job
- commit fewer criminal offences
- avoid claiming social welfare.

The researchers (Berrueta-Clement and others 1984) estimated that the long-term economic benefits to society of investing in preschool education were significant. For every dollar invested in preschool provision, there was a saving of seven dollars for improved quality of life for participants, their families and the community at large in later years. This pattern persisted when participants were aged 27 (Schweinhart and Weikart 1997). Sylva (1997) states that feeling in charge of your life is dependent on early shared control, and that there is a moral element inherent when children choose and negotiate. She argues that: 'The education environment shapes children's autonomy, decision making and feelings of control. These are dispositions which appear to pull children away from deviant pathways' (Sylva 1997: 93).

The researchers attributed these findings to a quality curriculum that includes the involvement of parents, an enriched developmentally appropriate programme and changed lives as a result of the programme. They also believed that the process of planning play led children to realise the relationship between actions and consequences, which persisted throughout adulthood, thus creating pro-social behaviour.

Further research by the High/Scope Foundation (Schweinhart and Weikart 1997) compared children following a free play and a direct instruction curriculum, with the High/Scope curriculum: 68 three and four year olds were assigned between these curricula models. Initial findings suggested that all groups functioned similarly in relation to intellectual and academic performance. At age 15, however, when the outcomes measured included community behaviour, children from the direct instruction group recorded more acts of misconduct than either the High/Scope or free play groups. They also had fewer social responsibilities in school than the other children. This trend persisted to age 23. The outcomes suggest that an overly formal curriculum has long-term consequences for children's social development. However, caution is essential in interpreting long-term studies such as these because many factors affect children's lives and development in the intervening years.

Vygotsky (1978), a social constructivist, believed that all children's learning takes place within a social context, thus learning appears on the social level before being internalised on the psychological plane. Vygotsky promulgated that all forms of play grow from the imagination, but that over time become rule governing. In imaginative play, children free themselves from reality and its constraints. In play, the relationship between imagination and rules changes over time from an initial emphasis on the imaginary situation to the later dominance of rules. Vygotsky understood role-play as a leading source of development in young children, but not the dominant form of activity. In play, children engage in imaginary situations, are free from situational constraints, create definitions of roles and subordinate themselves to rules that are created within the imaginary situation. There is a paradox in that free play is perceived as liberating children, yet implicit rules establish and maintain the play. Liberation and constraint coexist, because children are aware that if they do not act within their role then the play sequence may disintegrate.

Play, schema and representation

The work of Athey (1990) builds on that of Piaget. Her research team collected 5,000 observations of the free play of children from the age of two, analysis of which revealed several types of schematic behaviour or 'repeated patterns of behaviour' such as enveloping (wrapping things up), enclosing (putting a 'frame' around), connecting, separating, moving in circles, rotating objects, and transporting. The observations revealed that children's behaviours were not random but deeply purposeful. Langsted (1994: 32) concurs that 'the myth that children's activities are often chaotic and without direction has been exposed'. This research also highlights deeply intrinsically motivating behaviour that reflects children's prevailing interests and concerns. When adults recognise these patterns, understand why children carry them out and are aware of the possible links to later cognitive development, such as mathematical and scientific concepts, then they are in a position to support and extend the child's play. This knowledge challenges practitioners to reframe their thinking about children and the nature of their play. For example, a child who constantly moves materials and resources around the room may not be disruptive but engaged in exploring a transportation schema that provides knowledge about distance, time and mass. Children moving from one area of learning to another are often regarded as 'flitters'. Athey's theory presents a different hypothesis, which advocates that the child may be testing out the *same* idea, or schema, across all areas. The scenery may change but the plot is consistent. Through close observation and a sound knowledge base, adults will gradually increase their sensitivity to the child's actions and their meanings.

Children working within a schema need time to develop and practise ideas independently before combining them in more complex forms. Athey suggests that children will seek out others who are interested in the same schema. She also believes that these schemas are the curriculum within the child, and therefore the role of the adult is to respect, support and extend them. Her research concluded that children who experienced a curriculum that was responsive to their concerns in play showed significant gains on tests of intelligence, language comprehension, reading ability and vocabulary in contrast to a comparison group. These gains were not washed out during the first two years of primary school. An additional and unexpected outcome was that two years after the end of the project, younger siblings had a higher IQ than children in the experimental group. This was attributed to parents participating in an 'articulated pedagogical approach', which they then practised with their children at home.

Gura (1992) also identified the schematic concerns of children aged 3–6 years in their play with large wooden blocks. She found that after initial experience with the materials, children acted 'mathematically'. Curiosity drove children to study mathematical relations, to reflect on their problems and eventually come up with increasingly regularised but flexible methods of dealing with them. Children applied their learning in attempts to solve problems. Gura notes that curiosity, uncertainty and risk-taking, all of which were observed in blockplay, are features of scientific thinking. Spoken language and sharing were also important aspects of the play.

In play, children explore materials and use objects symbolically to 'represent' or stand for something that they are not. For example, a daisy can be used as an egg, or a leaf can represent a plate. Piaget (1985) describes symbolic play as developing through stages that become increasingly complex. They are:

- *Imitation* – the child reproduces a movement in response to an immediate experience.
- *Deferred imitation* – this is imitation after the model has gone (such as reproducing a tantrum that was observed a day or two earlier).
- *Symbolic play* – the child pretends to be asleep, or says 'meow' while moving a shell along the box. The actions and objects symbolise something other than what they are.
- *Drawing/graphic images* – an intermediate stage between play and the growth of a mental image.
- *Mental image* – the image is in the mind. There is no trace of it at the sensorimotor level.
- *Spoken language* – usually related to events that occur at the time.

These symbolic forms are a strong bridge between children learning through action and internalising abstract ideas in the mind. In free play children use all these symbolic forms when they dress up, draw, paint, make marks, build models, dance and talk.

Bruner (1981) also refers to representation but prefers to describe it as 'modes' rather than stages. He believes that the richest experience the child can have is to move freely between the different modes. The modes have much in common with Piaget's stages, but are not stage-related. They are:

- *Enactive* – the child knows the world through actions.
- *Iconic* – here children create images that are free from action. They draw, model and role-play.
- *Symbolic* – children translate actions and images into language.

The role of the adult is to give children time to work within these stages and modes within their play, but also to provide the materials so that children can repeat and explore their learning using different media.

Siraj-Blatchford and Siraj-Blatchford (2002) believe that children should be encouraged in their use of symbols. They advocate their use in communicating with others what they have done and understand. This is defined as metacognitive behaviour, because it enables children to reflect upon what they know, how they know it and what else they might usefully want to pursue in relation to it. The writers' comments are made within the context of research in science and technology with young children. They conclude that there are limitations to the child's autonomous exploration of materials and suggest that new techniques can emerge from instruction by an adult or another child who has previously learnt a skill. The writers refer to the instruction, engagement and involvement conditions for effective learning as evidenced in the 'instructional' approaches in Reggio Emilia and High/Scope. Those advocating these approaches may not subscribe to being 'instructional', although the authors acknowledge that inappropriate instruction can be 'devastating' for young children.

Whitebread and others' (2005) study explored the self-regulatory activities of 3–5-year-old nursery children and their metacognitive abilities. The authors define self-regulation as 'thoughts, feelings and purposive actions flexibly managed by the learner to achieve personal goals'. Of 705 observations, 281 were regarded as 'reasoned choices and decisions'. A feature of these was children's ability to develop their own ways of carrying out tasks. Some of these activities were child-initiated, others adult-initiated. The child-initiated activities promoted the highest metacognitive behaviours, followed by those that were adult-initiated, with those initiated between adult and child the lowest.

Play, health and well-being

Young children make up the most physically active group in society. Physical play is the first and most frequently occurring expression of play in young children (Hutt and others 1989). Evolutionary psychology tells us that our minds and bodies are adapted for the environment in which we evolved, from nomadic hunter-gatherers whose survival depended upon activity and physical exertion.

Bailey (1999: 47) informs us that: 'Play evolved as a process by which the body was prepared for the challenges likely to befall it'. From an evolutionary playwork perspective, the outdoor play environment provides opportunities for children to come and go as they please, and to establish links with other humans, species and systems.

Children can experience any of the indoor experiences in the outdoor environment; in addition they have the opportunity to develop coordination and control of their muscles. This is particularly important for children who are disabled. Ouvry (2003:9) suggests that children should be given the right context for play they can 'slip in and out of easily'. The outdoor environment provides unique opportunities for children to relive their experiences through movement, and learn about the natural world.

Cullen's (1993) study in Western Australia found that 82 per cent of children perceived outdoors as a social activity. They also thought outdoor play was to be undertaken without adult assistance. This may have been influenced by the fact that adults in the study rarely interacted with the children but adopted what Cullen describes as a monitorial role. This is a consistent theme throughout literature (Ouvry 2003). When adults did become involved, then stereotypical play was less likely to occur. Siraj-Blatchford (2001) emphasises that adults have a vital role in challenging cultural stereotypes that are adopted in play situations.

Article 24 of the United Nations Convention on the Rights of the Child affirms that children have a right to the highest level of health possible. A lack of spontaneous play opportunities has been cited as a causative factor in increased child obesity in England. Diseases such as coronary heart disease, obesity, hypertension (high blood pressure), hypercholesterolemia (high blood cholesterol), diabetes, back pain, posture problems, stress, anxiety and depression are witnessed in increasingly younger children (Biddle and Biddle 1989). It is increasingly accepted that physical play is necessary to address these situations.

The Health Education Authority (1998) recommended that children should do one hour of physical activity, of moderate intensity, a day. An observational study (Bailey and others 1995) of the level and tempo of 6–10 year olds found that the medium duration of any level of activity was just 15 seconds; bouts of intense activity lasted just three seconds. The children observed spent most of their time engaged in activities of low intensity interspersed with very short bursts of high intensity physical activity. Both boys and girls have been found to reduce their levels of physical activity between 6 and 18 years. The nature of the indoor and outdoor environments that young children typically inhabit may not, however, facilitate the intense physical activity that promotes the well-being described above. A national poll found that 80 per cent of parents believe that their children played outside less that they themselves did as children (Tweed 1999). The rate of decline has been particularly high in girls (Welshman 1997). Physical activity is a habit best acquired during childhood.

Physical activity has several benefits, including release from stress, confidence building and self-esteem. Physical activity also provides a domain in which relationships can be built, social cohesion promoted and opportunities for exploring difference provided. Physical activity can also be a tool for learning life skills such as risk-taking (National Playing Fields Association 2000).

Children have opportunities for play beyond that offered in the daily routines and timetables at school, for example at playtime and dinnertime. Tizard and others' work (1988) in inner London revealed that 28 per cent of the school day was taken up with dinnertime and playtime. Children's comments revealed that these times played a very important part in determining their general attitude to school. Attitudes differed according to gender and ethnic group. Dinner and playtimes were enjoyed by 68 per cent of pupils, but by boys more often than girls (75 per cent and 64 per cent respectively). Black boys enjoyed it the most (93 per cent) and white girls the least (53 per cent). The girls disliked the cold, being bullied and teased, and not having friends to spend the time with. Only four children gave negative reasons for enjoying playtime; for example to escape from lessons. Liking playtime was more closely related to enjoying the opportunity to run around and play games. Children did not enjoy the teasing and name-calling that went on in the playground and felt a lack of support from adults when this occurred. This was especially true of white girls.

Frost and Jacobs (1995) write passionately about play. They describe children's lives as increasingly dominated by schedules and believe this, with a concomitant decrease in public space for play, school playtimes and teachers trained in play leadership, is a cause for concern. School breaks and playtimes provide important opportunities for children to make and sustain friendships, and therefore school grounds have an impact on social inclusion.

School playtimes are frequently neglected aspects of school life. They can enhance social skills when children negotiate and take turns, or can be a negative experience when children experience exclusion. Lewis (1998) reports an initiative in a primary school, which sought to enhance children's experiences at breaks and dinnertimes. Lewis, a teacher, ensured that the community was involved in the project, and that children were central in the decision-making process. Traditional games and rhymes were taught to the children, adults committed themselves to being more participatory, and children were encouraged to bring objects from home to play with. The most frequent activities observed were of a social, then physical nature. Playing on structures was the most prevalent form of play (288 observations). There was a lack of success of traditional games, which was ascribed to lack of ownership of these by the children. Lewis found that older children (mainly girls in Key Stage 2) were more likely to play imaginative and traditional games with younger children. Older children policed and comforted younger children. The success of the project was attributed to the involvement of the children in the decision-making process.

In the past competitive sports have sometimes been regarded as creating unhealthy competition (Frost and Jacobs 1995; Bay-Hintz and others 1994). Therefore cooperative games have been recommended as the means of promoting cooperative behaviour and reducing aggression. Bay-Hintz and others (1994) observed a reduction of aggression and high levels of cooperation when children were in free play. Cooperative games increased sharing and encouraged strong peer relationships. They concluded that aggression in middle childhood is predictive of future antisocial behaviour and that the roots of aggression lie in the child's failure to learn and practise positive social behaviours. These affective responses to school are important. In conclusion, play promotes a more positive social disposition and attitude to school, not only in early childhood, but as children progress through primary school.

Play and risk

Concern with children's physical safety sits within a discourse of risks that 'threaten' children. But these concerns are set within a wider social framework of risk anxiety. This has resulted in increasing restrictions on children, who have fewer experiences of making decisions on their own, fewer opportunities to assess their own frontiers, and fewer opportunities to gain confidence and self-esteem. Being allowed to take risks, it has been argued, is an essential part of the ongoing process of becoming at home in the world. Gura (1992) has already reminded us that this is part of 'scientific' behaviour.

The general adoption of caution has had most effect in the sphere of children's lives. It is paradoxical that the emergence of a concern with children's rights coincides with the continuous erosion of the freedom that children have to play with each other. Parental responsibility has become associated with the willingness to supervise and chaperone children. Studies (such as O'Brien and Smith 2002) show how free outdoor play has been affected by parents' fears that hinge around traffic, strangers and drugs. The solutions that parents come up with are increased surveillance and organised activities. Parents, though, are aware that their children are not as 'free' as they were and they are also conscious that the children may be suffering from isolation and lack of exercise. Play has decreased as a result of increased anxiety in society.

It is argued that children themselves, however, not only need to take risks to learn (Lindon 2003), but they also seek them out when given the opportunity. Hughes (2001) describes risk as a legitimate expectation within playwork, although he differentiates between risk and danger. All children take risks, which they need to encounter and overcome. The risks should have real potential for physical learning.

Stephenson's (2003) study of two centres in New Zealand involving children under 5 years showed how children often chose to take physical risks they described as 'scary'. These activities involved attempting things not done before and things that gave them the feeling of being on the borderline of control because of speed or height, which led them to overcome their fear. Obviously some outdoor activities had more potential than others in this regard. Slides offered opportunities for both height and speed, and so did swinging. Climbing structures offered height. Children were observed to set up interactions that led to situations of self-induced fear.

In this study the teachers enjoyed being outdoors, were interested in physical play and had a liberal approach to supervision, which allowed children to find challenges that were experienced as risky but which did not put them in a position of hazard. The teachers' attitudes were, in fact, more important than the equipment itself. The researchers concluded that undertaking 'risky' activities was an integral part of the young child's drive to expand their physical prowess and so their independence.

The research concludes that there is, therefore, a need to:

- provide physically competent young children with a satisfying range of physically challenging experiences
- balance the requirement for safety with the need to provide physical challenges.

Without this, children get bored and grow up lacking confidence in their own physical ability. Physical confidence and competence have both been linked to general feelings of competence.

Risk-taking can be regarded as an intelligent behaviour, because creative people have been observed to place themselves in situations where they do not know what is going to happen.

This chapter presents a brief review of a number of issues that permeate the discussion of, and approaches to, play. These are:

- children's voices
- play and gender
- play and culture
- inclusive play.

Children's voices

Children are not always consulted on matters that closely concern them despite Article 12 of the UN Convention on the Rights of the Child, which states that: 'Parties shall assure to the child who is capable of forming his or her own views the right to express those views freely in all matters affecting the child.'

It is common in early years practice for adults to record and interpret children's play behaviours. However, these views may not necessarily represent children's perceptions and experiences. Scott (2000) suggests that there is a gulf between adults' interpretations of a child's understanding of a situation and the child's own perceptions. Children are one of the groups in society, alongside people with learning difficulties or mental health needs, who have been denied a voice, particularly in research. Since the late 1980s there has been increasing interest in listening to children's experiences and viewpoints. Cook and Hess (2005: 4) tell us that: 'To learn about a child's perspective adult researchers have to get beyond their own beliefs about a situation and listen to children in different ways.'

They elaborate by stating that adults have to adopt a position in which they listen and watch as well as relinquish some of their own power and predetermined agendas. Using the child's own photographic record as evidence, Cook and Hess (2005) found that having friends and feeling included was the most important aspect of school for children.

An evaluation by the authors of Early Excellence Centres (Cook and Hess 2001) aimed to gather the views and opinions of children, aged 4–5 years, on various aspects of their life in reception class. Questions to be explored included:

- What made children happy in the school and the Early Excellence Centre environment?
- What motivated them?
- How did they perceive the educational opportunities on offer?
- How did they participate in them?

Children took photographs of where they liked to play, their favourite toy and game, the places where they liked to work and wall displays that they liked. Through this process children revealed their own imperatives, which included:

- The importance of having playmates and the necessity of children meeting children.
- The importance of spaces and opportunities for play.
- The importance of doing something that they really want to do, rather than because others have given it some importance or have told them that it is important.

This project reminds us of the lived experiences of children, and reveals strong children who are able to express themselves on their own terms. When the adults tried to direct the interest of the children the authors noted that the action was less likely to be sustained. Offering an environment rather than determining the learning was more likely to be successful in motivating children.

Langsted (1994), a Danish writer, likewise argues that children have a right to be heard along with other users of early childhood services. This is in line with general principles laid down by the Danish Ministry of Social Affairs in 1990, which declared that 'Children must be listened to'. Langsted discusses the 'Children as Citizen's Project', which was established to increase children's influence on issues relevant to them. The project was carried out in five local authorities. Whereas most involved teenagers, some involved younger children. Langsted records what children from an early childhood centre fed back to staff after making observations of their preschool over two days. Among these was the statement that: 'It might be healthy to play but only if they wanted to – and nothing indicated that they all wanted to go out at the same time, just because adults thought they should' (Langsted 1994: 31). In response to these and other views, staff became more attentive to the needs of children, thus developing their sense of agency.

Langsted (1994) himself studied the lives of 24 kindergarten children in relation to their 'dual socialization' (page 36), at home and in the centre they attended when their parents were at work. They reported that the thing they liked about their centre was other children to play with, even though they reported that they could be teased by peers. The children perceived adults in the centre as making most choices, with the exception that children could decide who they played with. The children did not like some of the activities chosen by adults but felt that they had to carry these out. From the child's perspective, other children were by far the most important factor in determining quality, but toys, activities and adults were also important. The children liked the fun at kindergarten (more than at home) because there were lots of toys.

These projects give us some insights into children's feelings with regard to the experiences they have in childcare settings, the things that they like and those that are difficult for them. People, particularly peers, are of vital significance. Children enjoy play, but would like to have more choice in what they do and when they play, particularly in relation to the outdoor environment.

Play and gender

Between 30 and 36 months children begin to play predominantly with same-sex peers and this continues across childhood (Serbin and others 1977). Maccoby and Jacklin's (1987) longitudinal study indicated that preschool children spent nearly three times as much time playing with same-sex versus other sex partners. This ratio increased to 11 times by the age of six. The qualities of the play by boys and girls have been shown to be different. Boys' play tends to be rougher than girls' play and involves more active and forceful physical contact, fighting and taunting (Maccoby 1990). Boys showed greater rates of active forceful play than girls, particularly when in same-sex groups (Fabes and others 2003). Boys are more likely than girls to be in same-sex play but girls are more likely to be in same-sex dyadic or play in pairs (Fabes and others 2003). The two types of play provide different forms of interaction. Larger groups show more conflict and competition, dyadic play shows more sensitivity to others' needs.

In Busby's (1994) study carried out in a playgroup, gender differences also became apparent. At first, girls explored novel items such as forts and farms, but later played more consistently with dolls houses, prams, pushchairs and dressing up. The girls stayed longer than boys at activities that required fine motor skills. The boys preferred train sets, cars, garages and airports. Their pretend play often involved battles or superheroes such as Batman or Superman. They preferred more physical activity and were more aggressive. The children's role-play that Busby observed often involved different ages and both genders, but the dominant character was usually a boy.

Boys' hierarchical orders are more stable than girls', and girls' groups tend to emphasise cooperation by using communication skills. Martin and Fabes (2001) observed that the more frequently children play with same-sex peers the more frequently they engage in gender stereotyped activities. Cullen's (1993) work, however, highlights that when adults engage in outdoor play with children then it is less likely to become stereotyped. This may depend on the gender of the adult, because Sandberg and Pramling-Samuelson (2005) found that there are differences in participation in play by male and female teachers. In their study, female teachers did not participate in children's play as they were concerned not to change the nature of the play. Male teachers did participate, partly because they thought it would enable them to get to know the children better. Sometimes they had no purpose at all, they just wanted to participate. Male teachers participated in physical play. Women teachers saw this as a disturbing influence and tried to divert it with calm play. Sandberg and Pramling-Samuelson conclude that women teachers emphasise the importance of social development in play whereas male teachers emphasise physical development.

Typologies of aggression distinguish between acts that undermine physical dominance and those that subvert social acceptance (Crick and others 1997). Some researchers believe this distinction differentiates aggressive behaviour of boys and girls. Physical aggression is thought to be largely a feature of boys' behaviour (Crick 1999) and 'relational aggression', that is damaging a person's social relations or peer acceptance, is believed to characterise girls' aggressive behaviour (Crick 1997, 1999 and Crick and others 1996). In structured tasks, rates of physical aggression have been observed to decline and gender differences diminish compared with free play (Ostrov and Keating 2004).

An awareness of the nature and impact of aggressive behaviour during the early years is important in understanding the impact of antisocial behaviours on boys and girls and the impact of exclusion on individuals and groups. This awareness directs interactions and guides choice of resources and activities made by adults creating play environments.

Play and culture

Play is a culturally mediated activity that may take different forms in different groups. Recently, researchers have begun to explore the cultural dimensions of children's play in order to understand how these impact on the form and content of provision. Cross-cultural research suggests that children enact cultural-specific themes, reflecting activities and values that are important within specific communities. Universal dimensions of play for 2–4 year olds have been identified as the use of objects in pretend play and social interaction.

Curriculum models reflect the values and beliefs of a particular culture. In comparison to models in the United Kingdom at the time, Broadhead (2001) commented that curriculum models in other countries placed greater emphasis on young children's development than on a set of objectives to be achieved. Supporting practitioners in creating the right conditions for promoting development is also imperative. We now briefly consider some other approaches from beyond the United Kingdom, and, more recently from within.

Wales

The Welsh Assembly has made an explicit commitment to free play. Their play policy, produced in 2002, recognises the importance of play in children's development and affirms their intention to provide suitable environments for play in which children meet challenge, free from inappropriate risk. In the subsequent Wales Play Policy implementation plan they have committed themselves to:

- provide new funding specifically for play
- produce guidance as to what constitutes quality play opportunities
- involve children in the planning of play facilities
- introduce a new Foundation Phase (to cover Early Years and Key Stage 1) with a play-led approach to learning
- give support for the development of training resources on play for all school staff, including non-teaching staff and
- make school play facilities available to the community.

This new Foundation Stage in Wales is currently in its pilot phase and is being evaluated by Siraj-Blatchford (2005). The interim evaluation reveals that practitioners identified the most prominent strengths of the pilot as:

- a curriculum based on play, active and experiential learning
- a child-centred curriculum
- a broader, holistic, more relevant curriculum.

Reggio Emilia, Northern Italy

The first preschool school in Reggio Emilia was established after the Second World War. Historically there has been strong local investment by the municipality in the provision, which continues today. The principles that inform the establishments and the educational process are views of childhood. They are:

- *The child has rights*. The child is regarded as beautiful, powerful, competent, creative, curious and full of ambitious desires (Malaguzzi 1994). The belief that the child possesses rights is the foundation of the Reggio Emilia approach.
- *The child as an active constructor of knowledge*. The child occupies the primary role in their own education and learning. The child is believed to have an innate desire to discover and learn. 'Children are authors of their own learning' (Malaguzzi 1994: 55).
- *The child as a researcher*. In Reggio Emilia the child is encouraged to be a researcher through the context of projects or in-depth studies.
- *The child as a social being*. There is a strong emphasis on children's social construction of knowledge as developed through their relationships. Children communicate through language, but also in many diverse forms – the 'hundred languages of children' – and this is considered essential to bringing meaning to knowledge. Social relationships and the construction of knowledge often involve debate, discourse and conflict. These are encouraged within the provision in Reggio Emilia as a means to higher-level thinking (Hewett 2001). Within the schools there are no planned curricula or standards. The children, in collaboration with the teachers and each other, determine the course of their investigations and learning. Children are encouraged to express and interpret their knowledge in multiple ways.

Provision in Denmark

The provision in Denmark was influenced from the early 1800s by the work of NFS Grundvig, poet, philosopher, clergyman and historian. His tradition links education and democracy. He wanted a 'meaningful education' for all citizens to enable them to take part in a democratic society. In pursuit of this, emphasis is placed on history, literature and enabling individuals to enter into dialogue. Citizenship is another important element in the education system.

The Danish government supports a comprehensive provision of daycare based on the following principles (Langsted 1994):

- children's development, well-being and independence must be encouraged
- children must be listened to
- parents must have an influence
- centres must be regarded as a resource in connection with preventative work
- centres must be regarded as one of the neighbourhood's facilities for children.

In Denmark, early years workers are called social pedagogues. They have a broad training that focuses on developing communication skills, decision-making ability, flexibility and creativity. This training contains elements of working with young people, those who are disabled and those in different age groups. The pedagogues' training begins generally but then they specialise in an area of particular interest.

A feature of Denmark's provision is the forest school. The philosophy of forest schools is to encourage young people, through positive experiences and participation, to engage in activities in the outdoor environment. Through these activities they come to respect the things around them and take an interest in the effects of their actions on the world (Griffiths, C 2003).

This philosophy was first developed in Denmark for children under 7 years. The ethos was then introduced into the United Kingdom in the 1990s and has come to be regarded by many as an effective educational tool in a variety of settings. It is an innovative approach to outdoor activities and to learning. Advocates of the approach cite its effectiveness not only in terms of a respect for the environment, but also in helping to develop a range of skills central to educational and personal activity.

Visitors to Danish kindergartens often comment on the freedom that children exercise both in their play choices, use of the environment and the high levels of risk that they undertake.

Provision in New Zealand: Te Whariki

This curriculum approach is based on the following aspirations for children (Ministry of Education 1996: 9): 'To grow up as competent learners and communicators, healthy in mind, body and spirit, secure in their sense of belonging and in the knowledge that they make a valued contribution to society.'

The principles of Te Whariki are:

- *Empowerment* – the early childhood curriculum empowers children to learn and grow.
- *Holisitic development* – the curriculum reflects the holistic way children learn and grow.
- *Family and community* – the wider world of family and community is an integral part of the early childhood curriculum.
- *Relationships* – children learn through responsive and reciprocal relationships with people, places and things.

The principles are interwoven with strands and goals:

- Strand 1 – Well-being
- Strand 2 – Belonging
- Strand 3 – Contribution
- Strand 4 – Communication
- Strand 5 – Exploration.

We can see that approaches adopted in other countries have informed some elements of practice in the United Kingdom, most recently embodied in the Every Child Matters agenda (Department for Education and Skills 2003). What they all embrace is a view of children as strong, actively engaged in their own development and learning, and who have the right to have their voices heard on all issues concerning them.

Inclusive play

Inclusion is a process of identifying, understanding and breaking down barriers to participation and belonging (Early Childhood Forum 2003).

Play is central to the experience *of all* children, because through it they learn about the properties of objects and materials and how these can be used in creative ways both for pleasure and in practical problem-solving situations. They learn about themselves, how to make choices, take responsibility and develop a sense of agency when they influence their circumstances. They learn about others, their differences and similarities, social rules, as well as develop the skills to negotiate and resolve social conflicts. Play is also a means by which children can resolve inner conflicts and bring about emotional balance. However, for some children the opportunities to participate in play and avail themselves of these benefits may not be as prevalent as for others. These are children for whom their physical, social or cultural circumstance exclude them, either overtly or covertly, from participating fully in play. Those who tend to be most disadvantaged in accessing adequate play opportunities include children of asylum-seekers and refugees, Traveller children, children in homeless families, young carers, children of some ethnic minority communities, children in public care and disabled children.

Exclusion by peers brings serious risks to children's well-being and the development of their social competence (Stoller and others 1994), and can manifest itself in academic difficulties. These difficulties can have long-term consequences such as disaffection from school (Barrett 1989), mental health issues, and criminality in adolescence and adulthood (Utting and others 1993). Up to a half of 'disordered' adults have a history of problems in peer relationships, sometimes beginning when they are very young.

Harrist and Bradley (2003) describe how, to some extent, exclusion may be socially sanctioned by individuals as being necessary for the smooth functioning of the group.

There are a number of reasons for exclusion by peers (Harrist and Bradley 2003):

- children who behave in ways that their peers don't like
- children who are aggressive
- children who are socially withdrawn, disruptive, uncooperative, hyperactive, immature, lacking in pro-social skills
- children who are disliked for being 'different', such as belonging to a racial minority (particularly girls), being unattractive, having a disability.

Ladd and Coleman (1990) remind us that young children worry about peer relationships more than any other issue. Even if children change over time to a more positive disposition, negative reputations can be hard to change. Children's early peer problems are accumulative (Laine and Neitola 2004). Children with multiple or increasing problems in their social lives are more aggressive, inept in joining the group, and unable to comfort or notice others weaker than themselves (Stoller and others 1994). These children are particularly vulnerable. Olson (1992) found that early intervention is necessary or exclusion continues. Socially aversive exchanges can develop into active victimisation. Rejected children can become aggressive in response to their circumstances.

In addition to the normal stress experienced in growing up, peer exclusion may be the final stress that renders a child unable to cope (Henniger 1995). Whilst quality play experiences can keep stress at bay, too much stress can lead to 'play disruption' (Erikson 1976). The psychoanalytical perspective emphasises that if the child is unable to play, for whatever reason, this will impact on development and learning. It is a paradox that children need the social skills to form relationships in order to participate in cooperative play, yet at the same time social skills are developed through these social relationships.

Children who are suffering stress, abuse and illness

The very early relationships in which children find themselves impact on their development. Darwish and others (2001) found that maltreated children have significantly poorer skills in initiating interactions with peers and maintaining self-control, and a greater number of behaviour problems than peers who are not being maltreated. In their study, children with better social skills engaged in more interactive play. The experience of interacting with peers during play provided these children with important lessons regarding reciprocity, imitation and competition, which the authors consider to be the building blocks of social skills. Children who played alone often had underdeveloped social skills.

Lous and others (2000) explored the free play of depressed children and observed that they used less symbolic play, especially in play narratives (stories with figures that the adult starts and the child completes), and were more prone to fragmented behaviour as evidenced in a large number of switches from one type of play to another. In a later study (Lous and others 2002) comparing depressed and non-depressed 3–6 year olds in symbolic, pretend and fantasy play, they found that there was a drop in play for depressed children when a negative mood was introduced. They concluded that symbolic play may be threatening for very young children due to its potential to raise negative thoughts and feelings. They further cited neurobiological research that suggests that frightening and traumatic experiences of children who have disorganised attachments with their parents, and therefore stressful interpersonal situations, negatively affect the development of the brain, thus impairing the ability to cope with novel and stressful situations. The capacity of children to respond creatively in their daily interactions is constrained by the psychological environments within which they are placed. Stress limits the child's ability to play and thus the benefits available to them through it.

Ill-health likewise impacts on a child's quality of life and causes stress for the child and the family. As such, play can be important for children coping with the stress of illness. Gariepy and Howe (2003) compared 12 children with leukaemia with 12 without the illness. They found that the children with leukaemia:

- played less than the others
- engaged in a more limited variety of activities
- showed a significant relationship between self-reported stress and types of play, which was not true for the control group
- were engaged in more solitary play.

These findings support the view that children who are preoccupied and anxious may be unable to play at times, and are therefore deprived of an active and safe means of problem solving. There is a need to find ways to encourage such play. Providing ill children with more opportunities to play may be an important way of improving their quality of life.

Disabled children

Missuna and Pollock (1991) provide a health perspective on play. As occupational therapists they recognise that play is a primary productive activity for children, and therefore the drive to play is strong. For children who are physically disabled the ability to explore and interact is impaired. There is, therefore, an absence of information gathered through the senses and movement, which is crucial to discovering the properties of materials through epistemic play (Hutt and others 1989), or heuristic play (Goldschmied and Jackson 1994). Missuna and Pollock (1991) draw attention to the fact that children who are disabled can be additionally disabled because they are likely to become more dependent on their caregivers, and spend more time in their homes and in passive activities there. These circumstances can lead to an aggregation of social, emotional and psychological challenges. Play is a means of coping with anger, anxiety and frustration. For the child who is disabled there may be barriers to play, leading to deprivation. These barriers are:

- Caregivers (parents and teachers) who, although well meaning, may over-protect children or intervene too quickly in situations thus not allowing the child to gain independence and solve problems. Parents who are asked to function as a therapist with the child may, as a consequence, have less time and energy to engage in playful behaviour.
- Physical and personal limitations through lack of mobility to reach and grasp objects.
- Environmental challenge can lead to anxiety and frustration. Access to provision may be difficult or impossible due to barriers such as steps, narrow doorways and lack of space within which to manoeuvre. For the most part, buildings and playgrounds have been constructed to meet the needs of children who are not disabled.

- The physical structure of toys, which should be both familiar and novel. Toys should be sufficiently complex, with some thought given to their size, shape and weight.
- Factors in the child such as limited intrinsic motivation, lack of drive, decreased concentration and withdrawal.
- Social barriers. Through limited interaction with, or exclusion by, peers, the child who is disabled suffers further isolation. Children with physical disabilities may, therefore, have poorly developed social skills, which are the means by which they learn societal norms, the rules of behaviour and experiment with roles.
- Children who are receiving therapy have less time to play.

Each of these barriers has implications for the role of the adult. It is even more critical that adults should endeavour, in their relationships with children who are disabled, to avoid intervening too quickly, because through challenge, effort and struggle the child will develop increased motivation, a positive self-concept and more active participation. Careful thought should be given to the materials offered to the child, ensuring that they stimulate all the senses. The physical and emotional environment should provide safety and security alongside challenge and risk. The promotion of pro-social behaviour and inclusive relationships should be central to practice.

Approaches to foster inclusion

The goals of high quality programmes in the early years should be to enable all children to participate to the fullest extent (Bredekamp and Copple 1997).

As play is crucial for so many aspects of the child's development, adults must consider ways in which this can be offered and made accessible to all. Wolfendale (2001), while acknowledging that there are definitions and models of inclusion, recognises that these still vary. Some of these are discussed below.

Harrist and Bradley (2003) are critical of intervention models that are founded on a child deficit model based on changing the child, such as social skills training that provides direct instruction, reinforcement and social cognitive training in which children acquire cognitive and social skills by working with a peer helper. They consider that these models treat the symptoms without considering the reasons behind the behaviour. The authors adopt an approach described in Paley's (1992) work, in which she adopts a classroom rule that states explicitly that 'you can't say you can't play', based on the premise that school is for everyone and therefore no one should be left out. The approach was implemented with 10 kindergarten classes at three schools. The findings showed that target children reported that they liked to play with each other more, but had more concerns about their ability to make friends than children in a control group. The researchers acknowledge that this tension in their findings may be related to the data collection methods, and that their work did not address issues of gender or ethnicity.

Hestenes and Carroll (2000) studied 29 children, 21 of whom were typically developing and eight with delayed development or visual impairment. They found both typically developing children and those who were disabled chose similar activities, with most engrossed in gross motor development (one in two) and least with sensory play such as sand and water (fewer than one in three). In contrast, however, typically developing children engaged in more cooperative play and disabled children in more solitary play. Typically developing children spent less time interacting with peers who were disabled than expected, and vice versa. Key features in supporting play were the understandings that children had of disabled children and the extent to which they could predict and prepare for the things that would be difficult for them to deal with. The teacher's presence was also critical in initiating action and sustaining the play, although the precise features critical to success were not identified in this work.

Thomas and Smith (2004), while recognising that the development of play follows a predictable course for most children, pointed out that for children with autistic spectrum disorder, development is impaired, with play often appearing repetitive, sensory, isolated, concrete and lacking in imagination. Often there is only a limited range of toys used. These factors do not facilitate these children in playing with others, hence their social contact is limited, as are their play skills. Wolfberg (1999) maintains that without specific teaching, children with autistic spectrum disorder are unlikely to engage in functionally appropriate play. Thomas and Smith's (2004) study evaluates one preschool play intervention, Tabletop Identiplay, which combines a play script with tabletop mirroring. They found that:

- Children increased the amount of time they spent playing more appropriately with tabletop toys.
- Children learned and used all, or some, of the play sequence.
- Children played more purposefully with tabletop toys in free play sessions.
- Children used part of the taught play sequence, and two of the three children added creatively to it.
- Children spent an increased amount of time playing alongside, or with, other children.

When children play they are engaging in a complex process that affects all aspects of their development. The role of the adult in play is equally complex, because the adult must develop a repertoire of responses that are appropriate to each individual play situation, appropriate for children at different points in their development and responsive to a range of individual needs. The literature on play reflects different, and strongly held, perspectives on the nature of play and its place in children's lives. Each of these has a view on the role of the adult, guided by their own specific values and beliefs. The role of the adult will vary depending on the processes or products the adult perceives as being central to the play. As such, the role of the adult has been discussed at appropriate points in this review to make these contextually relevant. Adult roles may involve participation, observation, consultation, selecting materials and resources, involving parents, planning and writing policies. Of prime importance for play, however, are the relationships that the adult develops, which give children the confidence to act autonomously, make choices, follow their interests and interact with peers. In other words, creating a context in which children feel psychologically safe and socially included.

Sensitivity and attachment

The relationships within which children grow and develop have a major impact on their personalities, identity, developing social skills, and their dispositions to explore and learn. Children seek out social relationships. When these relationships are healthy, children become confident. The literature makes consistent links between the affective and cognitive aspects of play. The primary role of the adult therefore is to create a context that is both psychologically and physically safe, within which children feel secure, develop a sense of their worth and that of others, and develop the freedom and autonomy to explore and play. Although the physical environment should be clear of unexpected hazards, it should offer children opportunities to stretch and challenge themselves, taking risks appropriate to their stage of development.

From their very early days, babies and toddlers need opportunities to play freely. Adults should respond to their playful responses and be proactive in initiating these too. They should interpret and respond sensitively to the children's gestures and cues (Selleck 2001). In games, for example, the adult should aim to mirror the child's pitch and tone. In doing so the adult is creating synchrony. This sensitivity to the child's body language and cues in play is imperative in playwork.

During the early months the child is responsive to adults' emotions such as pleasure or depression (Field 1995). Responses to the child's emotional responses, such as smiling and crying, are critical in expressing sensitivity (Trevarthen 2005) and for building the emotional exchanges on which secure relationships are built. Selleck (2001) reminds us that in order to be effective in this aspect of practice, practitioners should get in touch with their own emotional and inner states of mind.

Strong emotional bonds or attachments (Ainsworth 1982; Meins and others 2001; Selleck 2001) are necessary for healthy development. The child's security is bound up in these for they meet the child's instinctive need to be close. Key factors in attachment sensitivity are acceptance, cooperation and responsive interactions with infants in the first year of life (Ainsworth and others 1971).

Meins and others (2001), who investigated attachment theory, found that maternal sensitivity is a factor in fostering securely attached children. Secure attachment develops from the mother's responsiveness to the infant's actions with objects and appropriate 'mind-related' comments. The authors describe 'mind-related' comments as those that treat infants as individuals with minds when responding to their child's direction of gaze, actions with objects and vocalisations. When mothers talk with their children about their feelings and how their behaviour impacts on others, and treat them as individuals with minds capable of complex relationships and events, this leads children to understand themselves and others, and therefore they are better able to take the role of a play partner. Parents with children who were securely attached imitated the child's vocalisation, were more likely to attribute meaning to the child's early vocalisations and encouraged autonomy, which is a key factor in exploratory and innovative play.

Adults working with children who are disabled should communicate and form bonds through the senses, using touch, texture, music, aromatherapy, signing and body language in their play exchanges.

Practitioners take on the role and responsibility of parents while children are in their care, and therefore the development of secure attachments is central to their work. Secure attachments through positive relationships give children a sense of value and belonging. Children who enjoy strong attachments with their mothers are more likely when older to be conciliatory with friends and enter elaborate shared fantasy bouts and conversations (Dunn 1993). The reverse is also true, however, for inconsistency and insensitivity can cause psychological damage and trauma, negative self-esteem and, later on, can result in an inability to tune in to others.

Children's early attachments influence the potential complexity of their play and social relationships in later years.

Observing children at play

Observation is a key tool for those working with young children. It opens their eyes to the competencies of young children, deepens their respect for them as learners (Drummond and Nutbrown 1996) and informs them about development and learning (Qualifications and Curriculum Authority 2000). Observations also inform adults about the child's interests, how long they persist in play, the patterns and rhythms of their play, and the partners who share their play. Through these observations, children who are in danger of exclusion can be identified and supported in accessing play materials and companions. Insights into the child's affective state can be gained through observing body language, and the skills of communication and language are also visible in play. Observations of children's free play reveal how children differentiate their own learning and set themselves challenges. Familiarity with children's interests in free play also provides information on which adult-initiated activities or visits can be based in order to make them relevant and meaningful to the child.

The work of Piaget and Isaacs used detailed observations to understand the learning processes. Working with children today is demanding on many levels. It requires astute and observant people to go beyond nurturing to develop effective practice (Selleck 2001). When observing, adults should place themselves in the child's shoes and ask how the event is being experienced by the child. Observation should be rigorous and reflective. When shared with others, insights are enhanced. Observation will sensitise adults to the play cues that children use when drawing peers and adults into their play.

Observations should be analysed within prevailing theoretical frameworks. Examples of these are provided in the report on implementing the Foundation Stage, by Adams and others (2004). Without explanatory power or interpretation and response by adults, observations have little meaning (Sutton-Smith 1979).

The conclusions reached by adults from their observations of children should be validated by discussion with the child, and where possible the parents or caregivers, each of whom will contribute their own unique insights. This is the principle utilised by Vivien Gussin Paley, the American early years practitioner, who records children's stories and uses these as the focus for discussion. These insights will give a voice to children and, in turn, enhance the quality of their experience.

UNICEF's response to Article 12 of the United Nations Convention on the Rights of the Child (http://unicef.org.index.php) has identified the need for adults to:

> ... create spaces and promote processes designed to enable and empower children to express views, to be consulted and to influence decisions ... the child's evolving capacity represents just one side of the equation: the other involves adults' evolving capacity and willingness to listen to and learn from their children, to understand and consider the child's point of view, to be willing to re-examine their own opinions and attitudes and to envisage solutions that address children's views.

This in turn guides in the choice of resources for the environment that will support and extend children's play.

Interacting with children in play

The extent to which the adult interacts with children during their free play will vary depending on the circumstances. One school of thought advocates non-intervention as an appropriate means of interacting, because a more interactive approach interferes with the child's play (Pellegrini and Galda 1993). For example, during play with the 'treasure basket' Goldschmied and Jackson (1994) establish the adult's role as one of 'emotional anchorage', a quiet reassuring presence whose body language encourages the child to explore, yet does not actively participate. This enables the child to make his or her own choices concerning the materials and how they are used.

Adults are advised against premature intervention in children's play as this robs them of the opportunity to make mistakes, learn from them, solve problems creatively and negotiate solutions to social conflict (Hohmann and Weikart 1995). Missuna and Pollock (1991) found this is to be true particularly when working with children who were disabled, because when the adult solves problems and intervenes inappropriately the child can become doubly disabled as a result of dependency and loss of power and control.

Therefore, in many situations the adult should act as a non-participant in the play, yet actively observe and note what children are doing to develop understanding of the child's affective state, intellectual concerns and physical and social skills, friendships and abilities. If adults are directly involved in play, they may inadvertently transmit their values, rules and traditions to children.

The literature, however, makes a strong case for a more structured adult role when playing with children who have a lack of mobility or insufficient fine motor skills to enable them to access objects independently (Missuna and Pollock 1991). Modelling play with objects, encouraging play with others to develop their social skills (Thomas and Smith 2004), and helping children to initiate and sustain their play (Hestenes and Carroll 2000) add to the repertoire of the adult in this context. When adults play with children they stimulate their senses. Disabled children cannot always indicate when they are bored (Brodin 1999), and therefore the adult should also observe closely and develop sensitivity to children's individual needs.

In other situations the adult must be available to join children in their play when they are invited to do so – for example, in role-play when asked to take the role of the patient in the hospital. On other occasions the adult might choose to play alongside children when they are painting, drawing, modelling or building with bricks, with the hope that they will be drawn into the conversation and play. In this way the adult respects the child's right to be in control of the action. Broadhead's (2001) work describes how children in some play situations draw adults in to resolve conflicts, but when engaged in more complex play they are able to resolve altercations and solve problems themselves. Therefore, children are active in drawing in the adult to support them when it is necessary but work towards having mastery over all aspects of their situations, and will refuse support when they feel in control.

A Vygotskian approach would advocate that adults actively engage with children in an sensitive manner, as there are benefits in supportive and responsive interactions. Adams and others (2004) attributed the impoverished learning environment and a lack of complex play they observed to the lack of interaction from adults. In Head Start Programs in the United States teachers and assistant teachers were observed to be highly involved in children's play. They spent the majority of their time helping children get involved in, and facilitating, this play. However, they were less likely to become involved in dramatic play, and the quality of the talk between teachers and children was neither rich nor stimulating. These findings are significant, because children are more likely to play where there is an adult present, and the quality of talk is an important element of caregiver–child interaction that predicts cognitive and language skills (NICHD Early Childhood Research Network 1996).

The adult does have an active role in challenging in a sensitive, yet fair, way any stereotypical or inappropriate behaviour that arises, both within and without the play situation. Children's self-esteem and identity are fostered through the types of interactions and relationships they have with adults and peers. Adults are role models for children, and therefore they have the power to influence values, attitudes and behaviour (Siraj-Blatchford 2001). For example, if children from some groups are treated differently by adults, their peers will learn to respond in the same way. Children should learn about similarities between groups as well as differences. They should learn that individuals within a group are not necessarily representative of the whole group. Comments that reflect stereotypes or prejudice should be dealt with through talk, explanations given as to the unacceptability of a comment and the feelings of the children discussed. Correct information should be shared and support given to the children involved, primarily the child who is hurt, but not neglecting the child who has caused the offence, albeit unwittingly.

With regard to social exclusion in play, Paley's (1992) work as explored by Harrist and Bradley (2003) introduced a rule that did not permit children to exclude peers from their play. This is a direct and somewhat radical intervention available to practitioners, the appropriateness of which should be judged for each setting individually. The benefits of this approach should be weighed against the benefits children gain from learning how to develop strategies to enter into the play context.

Feinburg and Minders (1994) highlighted three areas that are important in the social-affective domains:

- Helping children to express and deal with their own feelings and those of others.
- Fostering in children an understanding of similarities and differences among people and respect for these.
- Developing the skills for forming friendships such as reading the behaviour of others, initiating contact, handling rejection and negotiation.

When children and adults have authentic conversations with children during their exploration and play, children learn to name objects, describe situations, explain behaviour and phenomena, predict a course of action and express their feelings. Observations of talk between children and teachers reveal that it is the teachers who most frequently initiate the conversations and usually dominate them. Tizard and Hughes (1984), observing children's talk at nursery and at home with parents, reported that the opposite was true when children dialogued with their parents. In the home context, children most often initiated conversations and the adults responded to, and sustained them. Fundamental to these exchanges were the shared experiences of parents and children, such as visits to their grandparents and walks in the park. Conversations also flowed naturally when the adult and child were engaged together in 'real-life' situations, such as dusting and making meals. In other words, authentic conversations occur in real-life contexts that make sense to the child. Conversational exchanges are more likely when adults are genuinely interested in children's thoughts and ideas, give them time to initiate conversations and avoid closed, test questions that are focused on fixed outcomes.

Athey (1990) suggests that adults' conversations with children tend to focus on the *content* of their products (whether their drawing or painting is a car, elephant, house or teddy bear), and not the *forms* (straight lines, circles, diagonal lines and concentric circles). She believes that it is the *forms* that children are more interested in, and when adults reflect back to children their understanding of this – for example by saying 'I see that you have used a lot of circles in your picture' – then children understand that they have been understood and that their interests have been valued and respected.

Supporting interactions between peers is another important function of the adult during play. The adult can refer children to one another so that, through talk and social interaction, they can learn about themselves and one another. When children share with others what they have done, or plan to do, they are organising their thoughts, developing communication skills and availing themselves of the insights of others. They begin to understand how and why they do things and consider alternative and more effective courses of action.

The role of the adult is to support and extend learning through skilful open-ended questioning, authentic conversational exchanges and referring children to one another to find solutions to problems. The timing of these interventions is crucial so that they neither intrude upon nor frustrate or terminate the play. The adult acts as a scaffold, enabling children to move into new areas of understanding and development.

Bearing all of the above in mind, Selleck (2001: 81) warns that it is possible to over stimulate children: 'there is no doubt that children respond to play opportunities and fail to thrive when deprived of touch, holding and playful companionship. But it seems that the other extreme – over stimulation, bombarding babies with objects, colour or unremitting attention can be just as unhelpful.'

There is also the risk that some children who are disabled are constantly faced with the training situation in which play is used to train them in a particular function, or as a means of unremitting assessment.

Resourcing the environment

The environments in which play takes place are important. They are central to the way in which play is allowed to develop and flourish (Abbott and Nutbrown 2001). These environments include indoors and outdoors. Adults are responsible for choosing materials and resources, based on their knowledge of child development and individual children's interests and abilities.

The outdoor environment should be an extension of the indoor environment in that anything that is offered indoors can reasonably be offered outdoors, and the outdoor environment can foster all aspects of the child's development. Notwithstanding, the outdoor environment provides children with unique opportunities to explore nature and test their gross motor skills. Esbensen (1987) recommends that the outdoor play space should be zoned to facilitate children's diverse interests. Some zones would facilitate climbing apparatus, others social interaction, yet others sensory or socio-dramatic play. Dividing space into areas dedicated to specific types of play ensures that noisy or physical play does not intrude into quieter social areas, although children do have flexibility to move equipment and develop their play over a number of areas. Paths, hills, patches to grow flowers and vegetables, and wild areas all enlarge the potential for rich, imaginative and exploratory play. They also meet children's evolutionary needs of associating with the past, developing creativity and mastery, and positively impacting on brain development (Hughes 2001).

In order to support children's exploration in play there should be a wide range of materials of different textures, colours, shapes and sizes. There should be materials that are familiar to the child and those that are novel in order to present challenge. The current preponderance of commercial products made from plastic in some settings should be mediated by natural materials that provide a richer source of sensory information.

Materials should be accessible to the children so that they can choose the resources that best suit their purposes. The materials that best support children's creativity are open-ended. Their adaptability and lack of explicit function provokes children's imagination and creativity. Resources chosen for children who are disabled should be developmentally appropriate and flexible in use – for example they should include things that can be held in the hand or by feet.

Ouvry (2003) reminded us that the role of the adult in the outdoor environment should be as active as that in the indoor environment. Cullen's (1993) work showed that when adults do become involved in outdoor play then stereotypical play is less likely to occur.

Children need time to repeat and practise their play behaviours. Children therefore need time to repeat their actions. Cullen's work draws attention to the fact that the management and organisation of timetables can restrict children's opportunities for outdoor play. This is equally true of play indoors. Adults should ensure that children have time to become engaged in complex play and have some control over how and when this is terminated. Repetition leads to more complex combinations of materials, ideas and higher levels of learning. When adults are confident in their understanding of this they will not be concerned about repetitious behaviour and consequently avoid the temptation to move children on to gain experience in other areas of learning.

The manner in which resources are stored and available to children supports or hinders their play. These resources should be readily accessible to children and should reflect cultural diversity. The latter has been an aspect of provision that has traditionally not been well catered for in early years settings (Sylva and others 1999) except in combined centres and some nursery schools. Books, play materials, such as dressing up clothes and utensils for the home area, and posters should portray positive images of gender, race, class and disability.

Rutter (2002) suggests that play helps the children of refugee families to make sense of the stresses and changes that they experience. They gain confidence through interaction and exploration and are given the possibility of regaining trust that has been lost in adults and others. In order to do this they need space, toys, time and empathy. Small figures provide an outlet for children to express their 'stories'. Rutter also advocates:

- Sensory and exploratory play.
- Drama/puppetry to play out feelings.
- Painting and drawing.
- Opportunities for free play, particularly in home corners to express and interpret stressful events.
- Stories that contain the theme 'being new', which can be acted out. In doing so, values such as sharing and justice and ethnic diversity can be explored.
- Telling stories from the children's own countries of origin.
- Celebration of faiths and festivals.
- Celebration of children's home languages reflected on posters, labels, books, inclusion of parents and ideally by the presence of a bilingual worker.

The roles that adults adopt in children's play can be numerous. The success of these roles lies in adults' understanding of children and play, the range of strategies they have available and their flexibility in applying these strategies.

From the literature it is evident that free play is a highly motivating process in which children have participated across cultures and throughout history. As such, it is incumbent upon those involved in working with young children to gain the best insights possible into the meanings free play carries for children, and the contribution that it makes to their development and learning. At the same time it must be recognised that, due to its complexity, play may defy the very act of definition, and any attempt to do so leaves us open to the criticism that we are guilty of the pedantic intellectualising of play (Vygotsky 1978). Children live with the paradox of play and we may have to do likewise.

There are many different perspectives in the play literature, not all of which sit comfortably with one another. The differences in some cases lie in the degree of emphasis on one aspect of play to the detriment of another. In other cases the differences are more fundamental. There are some tensions inherent in the literature. For example, the juxtaposition of play as a connection to our evolutionary past, and play as a fairly recent construct created by society to explain specific child behaviours.

Another tension lies in understanding how adults should respond to children's play, if indeed they should at all. In early childhood practice, what was described in the past as the laissez-faire approach, in which adults saw their role as providing an environment for the 'unfolding' of development and learning, has been replaced by an interactionist approach, which advocates active support and extension of play. In settings that are working with children in the Foundation Stage, there is the further tension of balancing process and product in a climate in which there is inspection, outcomes and goals.

What is evident is that at present there is an increasing interest in play, and an increasing wealth of experience and research growing in the field. These studies come from different theoretical perspectives, all of which have a common interest in play. It would seem to be an appropriate time for these different disciplines to draw together to share understandings and negotiate new meanings in play. Working together, with respect for the professional knowledge and skills of others in this field, will create a stronger forum for children's play.

Within the present literature there is evidence that free play contributes to the child's development and learning in the physical, social, emotional and cognitive domains. Children's actions, relationships, changing behaviours and development of skills evidence this. While being an essential element for learning in young children, free play however is not the only way in which children learn. Sometimes they learn by being told. This learning usually takes place in a context in which the information shared is in response to questions that children ask, and therefore they are receptive to it. Children also learn by observing. This makes the role model adopted by those who have close relationships with children of crucial importance. Children identify with, and perpetuate, the attitudes, beliefs, cultural assumptions and prejudices of those around them. When these are emotionally affirming and socially acceptable the child benefits, when they are not then the child faces new learning when entering the wider social group. Children also learn from experiences that are outside their free play. For example, taking part in visits, having visitors in the home or setting, sharing household chores, and experiencing illness all contribute to children's developing understanding of the world.

Play that is planned, initiated and structured by adults can also create new learning in children. This is more effective when skilled adults plan activities that are relevant to the child, and during which their interaction is tailored and responsive to the child. Through these activities, adults help children to make connections between previous and new knowledge.

Research, such as that by Berrueta-Clement and others (1984) and Schweinhart and Weikart (1997) highlight the benefits of planned child-initiated play to families and communities through increased social responsibility and reduced antisocial behaviour. When children develop good health, mental well-being and positive social relationships through play, the prediction for the long term is that these dispositions will reduce future demands on carers and the health service, and thus enable children to make positive contributions to society through employment.

Secure attachments to adults, plus the opportunity to engage in social play when young, may go some way in ameliorating antisocial and delinquent behaviour later on. It would be simplistic, however, to believe that play is the panacea for all social problems.

Through free play, children learn about cultural identity and inclusion. In an increasingly culturally diverse nation, this knowledge cannot be developed too soon. Not all children, however, have equal access to play or play facilities. This may be due to adults' lack of awareness of its importance, restricted availability and resources, difficulties in physical access or fear of exclusion from the dominant group. In these situations adults are to be advocates for the rights of all children to play and leisure, to participate fully in society as well as have their voices heard. Play can potentially contribute to social cohesion.

Early years ideology, however, is not always translated into practice. This is problematic because the work of Wood and Attfield (1996) and Adams and others (2004) highlights the tension between rhetoric and reality in relation to play. Not all practitioners provide the play opportunities for children that they would wish to offer. They perceive play to be of low value to politicians, and often to their colleagues in different phases of education. Testing, and a curriculum that is goal-oriented affect their pedagogy. They spend little time supporting children in their play but invest time in activities that they choose for children. Not all practitioners are confident in using play as a tool for learning. They are not able to link pedagogy, play and children's learning. While recognising that these findings reflect the practice of a relatively small sample of teachers, the message is a salient one because it suggests that initial and subsequent training of teachers does not make this a priority.

Finally, the innovative approach in Wales, to a play-based curriculum for children up to seven years, may have consequences for children in England in the future. The transition between the Foundation Stage and Key Stage 1 in England can present challenges for children if the principles underpinning practice differ. Children moving into Key Stage 1 are very young and many of their counterparts in European countries and now in Wales are still experiencing a play-based curriculum at this age.

Key questions

There are issues arising in this literature review that raise questions for us to consider:

- If we are to ensure that children have the right to play as defined in the United Nations Convention on the Rights of the Child, 1989, should there be more emphasis on child development and the role of play, including free play, in development and learning in the training of all adults working with young children?
- Should local authorities make it a priority to provide training that highlights the benefits of free play, and the strategies to support this, for all staff in their early years settings?
- Would there be benefits in drawing together professionals such as playworkers, play therapists, occupational therapists and educationalists to share their expertise with one another and inform initial and in-service training on play?
- As there is much less known about the free play of 5–7 year olds, should further research be carried out to investigate their experiences both within their school contexts and in the community.
- Should practitioners be actively recruited as researchers on such projects, because they are in the best position to understand the issues, disseminate these to others and promote change?
- Should there be further research investigating risk-taking and play, the play experiences of the children of asylum-seekers and Travellers, and comparative studies of free play and adult-initiated play?
- Where can small groups find funding to support the development of stimulating outdoor areas in early years settings?

One further important area for future discussion is the terminology used to describe and discuss play. There are assumptions that there is a common understanding of the terminology within and between professions. However, the literature – and discussion with those involved in children's play – suggest that the terms 'free', 'spontaneous', 'child-initiated', 'planned', 'purposeful', and 'structured' play are ill-conceptualised and interpreted in disparate ways. This inhibits communication between those working to provide children with opportunities for play. It may be the right time, while maintaining professional identity, to establish a more coherent inter-professional approach to children's play.

Methodology

1. This literature review was commissioned in May 2006 and carried out between May and July of the same year. Play England circulated the first draft of the work to their members during August for responses. The review was redrafted in September in the light of these responses. During October the review was prepared for publication.

2. The following databases were used:
   - ASSIA
   - Australian Education Index Database (1975 to date)
   - British Education Index Database (1975 to date)
   - ERIC (1996 to date)
   - HSWE Database – indexing journals held in Coach Lane Library, University of Northumbria
   - IngentaConnect
   - Northumbria University Library at Coach Lane Campus
   - ZETOC Database

3. The following websites were searched:
   - ATL
   - DfES
   - Google
   - Institute of Education
   - MEDAL
   - Medline
   - Social Research Online
   - The Play Council
   - Welsh Assembly Government website

4. Search terms used were:
   - Abused children
   - Autonomy
   - Child-initiated activities
   - Childhood needs
   - Children
   - Disabled children
   - Disadvantaged children
   - Free play
   - Homeless children
   - Independent learning
   - Learning difficulties
   - Learning disabilities
   - Maltreated children
   - Neglected children
   - Parental involvement
   - Parents
   - Play

- Poor children
- Preschool children
- Pretend play
- Refugees
- Special needs
- Street children
- Travellers

5. Libraries:
- Northumbria University, Coach Lane Campus
- The Children's Play Information Service

6. Further sources of information were the works of:
- Early Years pioneers.
- Learning theorists – Freud, Piaget, Vygostsky and Bruner.
- Well-known and respected writers in the field of Early Childhood.
- Curricula approaches from abroad – High/Scope. Reggio Emilia, the forest schools in Scandinavia.

7. Research documents were analysed using the analytic framework set out in Appendix B.

8. Articles, chapters in books and websites were analysed using the analytical framework set out in Appendix B.

A decision was made to incorporate information from as many different perspectives as possible in the final document in order to present as broad a picture as possible on the subject.

Priority was given to articles in refereed journals because these were regarded as having undergone initial peer scrutiny. Every effort was made during the writing of the review to provide information regarding the methodology of research in a manner that did not interfere with the coherence of the document.

Although some articles focused on children aged birth–3 years, the majority reflected the experiences of children aged 3–5 years. There was a dearth of information on free play for children aged 5–7 years.

The literature reflected predominantly an 'education' focus, with a central theme of play as a learning process.

Analytical frameworks

i Research documents

Aims	Research group	Research methods

ii Articles, books and websites

Title, author, date	Currency of literature: Research ®, article in referred journal (ARJ) (RJ) article (A), chapter in book (CB) book (B) website (W)	Main themes and insights

Abbott, L and Nutbrown, C (2001) *Experiencing Reggio Emilia: Implications for Preschool Provision.* Buckingham: Open University Press.

Adams, S, Alexander, E, Drummond, MJ and Moyles, J (2004) *Inside the Foundation Stage Recreating the Reception Year.* London: Association of Teachers and Lecturers.

Ainsworth, MDS (1982) 'Attachment: Retrospect and prospect', in Parkes, CM and Stevenson-Hinde, J (eds) *The Place of Attachment in Human Behavior.* New York: Basic Books.

Ainsworth, MDS, Bell, SM and Stayton, DJ (1971) 'Individual differences in strange-situation behaviour of one year olds', in Schaffer, HR (ed) *The Origins of Human Social Relations.* London: Academic Press.

Alexander, R, Broadfoot, P and Phillips, D (1999) *Learning from Comparing: New Directions in Comparative Educational Research: Contexts, Classrooms and Outcomes.* Oxford: Symposium.

Athey, C (1990) *Extending Thought in Young Children: A Parent–Teacher Partnership.* London: Paul Chapman Publishing.

Bailey, DB, McWilliam, RA, Buysse, V and Wesley, PW (1995) 'Inclusion in the context of competing values in early childhood education', *Early Childhood Research Quarterly,* 13(1), 27–47.

Bailey, R (1999) 'Play, health and physical development', in David, T (ed) *Young Children Learning.* London: Paul Chapman Publishing.

Ball, C (ed) (1994) *Start Right: The Importance of Early Learning.* London: Royal Society for the Encouragement of Arts, Manufacturers and Commerce.

Barrett, G (1989) *Disaffection from School: The Early Years.* Falmer, Sussex: Falmer Press.

Bartoletti, S (1996) *Growing Up in Coal Country.* Boston, MA: Houghton Mifflin.

Bay-Hinitz, AK, Peterson, RF, Quilitch, HR (1994) 'Cooperative games: A way to modify aggressive and cooperative behaviors in young children', *Journal of Applied Behavior Analysis,* 27, 435–446.

Bennett, N and Kell, J (1989) *A Good Start? Four Year Olds in Infants' Schools.* Oxford: Blackwell Education.

Berrueta-Clement, JR, Schweinhart, IJ, Barnett, WS, Epstein, AS and Weikart, DP (1984) *Changed Lives: The Effect of the Perry Preschool Program on Youths Through Age 19.* Monographs of the High/Scope Research Foundation, 8. Ypsilanti MI: High/Scope Press.

Berry, CF and Sylva, K (1987) *The Plan–Do–Review Cycle in High/ Scope: Its Effects on Children and Staff.* Oxford: Department of Social and Administrative Studies University of Oxford.

Biddle, S and Biddle, G (1989) cited in Bailey, R (1999) 'Play, health and physical development', in David, T (ed) *Young Children Learning.* London: Paul Chapman Publishing.

Bilton, H (2002) *Outdoor Play in the Early Years* (second edition). London: Hodder and Stoughton.

Bowlby, J (1969) *Attachment and Loss, Vol 1: Attachment.* New York: Basic Books.

Boyce, ER (1938) *Play in the Infants' School: An account of an educational experiment at the Raleigh infants' school, Stepney, London, January 1933–April 1936.* London: Methuen and Co Ltd.

Bredekamp, S and Copple, C (1997) *Developmentally Appropriate Practice in Early Childhood Programs.* Washington, DC: National Association for the Education of Young Children.

Brierley, J (1994) *Give Me a Child Until He is Seven.* Falmer, Sussex: Falmer Press.

Broadhead, P (2001) 'Investigating sociability and cooperation in four and five year olds in reception class settings', *International Journal of Early Years Education*, 9, 1, 23–35.

Brodin, J (1999) 'Play in children with severe multiple disabilities: Play with toys – A review', *International Journal of Disability, Development and Education*, 46, 1, 25–34.

Brown, F (2003) *Playwork Theory and Practice.* Buckingham: Open University Press.

Bruce, T (2001) *Learning through Play: Babies, Toddlers and the Foundation Years.* London: David Fulton Publishers Ltd.

Bruce, T (2005) 'Play, the universe and everything', in Moyles, J (ed) *The Excellence of Play.* Buckingham: Open University Press.

Bruner, J (1981) 'What is representation?', in Roberts, M and Tamburrini, J (eds) *Child Development 0–5.* Edinburgh: Holmes McDougall.

Bruner, J (1996) *The Culture of Education.* Harvard University Press Cambridge, Massachusetts and London, England.

Bruner, JS, Jolly, A and Sylva, K (1985) *Play: It's Role in Development and Evolution.* Harmondsworth: Penguin Books.

Busby, J (1994) 'The importance of free play: A research study of free play time in a playgroup', *Early Years*, Autumn, 15, 1, 54–58.

Children's Workforce Development Council (2006) *Early Years Professional National Standards*. Leeds: Children's Workforce Development Council.

Christensen, P and James, A (eds) (2000) *Research With Children: Perspectives and Practices*. Falmer, Sussex: Falmer Press.

Cohen, D (1993) *The Development of Play* (second edition). London: Routledge.

Cook, T and Hess, E (2001) *A Report on Events, Play, Toys, Adults and Children in the Classroom in a Reception Class*. Newcastle: Northumbria University.

Cook, T and Hess, E (2005) *Children's Voices*. Paper developed from a SureStart Early Excellence Evaluation. Newcastle: Northumbria University.

Crick, NR (1997) 'Relational and overt aggression in preschool', *Developmental Psychology*, 33, 35, 579–588.

Crick, NR (1999) 'Relational and physical forms of peer victimisation in preschool', *Developmental Psychology*, 35, 376–385.

Crick, NR, Bigbee, MA and Howes, C (*1996*) 'Gender differences in children's normative beliefs about aggression', *Child Development*, 67, 1003–1014.

Cullen, J (1993) 'Preschool children's use and perceptions of outdoor play areas', *Early Childhood Development and Care*, 89, 45–56.

Darwish, D, Esquivel, GB, Houtz, JC and Alfonso, VC (2001) 'Play and social skills in maltreated and non maltreated preschoolers during peer interactions', *Child Abuse and Neglect*, 25, 13–31.

Department for Education and Employment (1999) *Sure Start: a guide for second wave programmes*. London: Department for Education and Employment.

Department for Education and Skills (2003) *Every Child Matters: Change for Children*. Norwich: The Stationery Office.

Department for Education and Skills (2004) *The Five Year Strategy for Children and Learners*. London: The Stationery Office.

Department of Education and Science (1990) *Stating with Quality: The Report of the Committee of Inquiry into the Quality of Educational Experience Offered to 3 and 4 year olds Chaired by Mrs Angela Rumbold CBE MP*. Norwich: The Stationery Office.

Department of Health (2004) *The National services framework for children, young people and maternity services*. London: The Stationery Office

Donaldson, M (1978) *Children's Minds*. London: Fontana Press.

Drummond, MJ and Nutbrown, C (1996) 'Observing and Assessing Young Children' in Pugh, G (ed) *Contemporary Issues in the Early Years Working Collaboratively for Children* (second edition). London: National Children's Bureau Early Childhood Unit.

Dunn, J (1983) 'Sibling relationships in early childhood', *Child Development,* 54, 787–811.

Dunn, J (1993) *Young Children's Close Relationships: Beyond Attachment.* Newbury Park, CA: Sage.

Early Childhood Forum (2003) *Quality in Diversity in Early Learning: A Framework for Early Childhood Practitioners* (second edition). London: National Children's Bureau.

Early Years Curriculum Group (2002) *Onwards and Upwards: Building On the Foundation Stage.* Oxford: Early Years Curriculum Group.

Esbensen, S (1987) *An Outdoor Classroom.* Ypsilanti, MI: High/Scope Press.

Erikson, E (1950) *Childhood and Society.* New York: WW Norton.

Erikson, E (1976) 'Play and cure', in Schaefer, C (ed) *The Therapeutic Use of Child's Play.* New York: Jason Aronson.

Fabes, RA, Martin, CL and Hanish, LD (2003) 'Young children's play qualities in same-, other- and mixed-sex peer groups', *Child Development,* 74, 3, 921–932.

Fagen, R (1981) *Animal Play Behaviour.* New York: Oxford University Press.

Family and Work Institute (1996) *Rethinking the Brain: New Insights Into Early Development.* Chicago: Family and Work Institute.

Feinburg, S and Minders, M (1994) *Eliciting Children's Full Potential.* California: Wadsworth.

Field, TM (1995) 'Psychologically depressed parents', in Bornstein, MH (ed) *Handbook of Parenting Vol 4, Applied and Practical Parenting* (pp.85–99) Mahwah, NJ: Lawrence Erlbaum Associates.

Frost, JL (2005) 'Lessons from disasters: Play, work and the creative arts', *Child Education, 82, 1,* 2–8.

Frost, JL and Jacobs, PJ (1995) 'Play deprivation: A factor in juvenile violence', *Dimension of Early Childhood,* Spring, 14–20.

Gariepy, N and Howe, N (2003) 'The therapeutic power of play: Examining the play of young children with leukaemia', *Child Care, Health & Development,* 29, 6, 523–537.

Garvey, C (1991) *Play* (second edition). London: Fontana Press.

Goldschmied, E and Jackson, S (1994) *People Under Three Young Children in Day Care.* London: Routledge.

Goleman, D (1996) *Emotional Intelligence: Why It Can Matter More Than IQ*. London: Bloomsbury Paperbacks.

Griffiths, C (2003) *The Forest School: SureStart Evaluation*. Newcastle: Northumbria University.

Griffiths, J (2003) 'Do little children need big brains?' *Early Education*, Summer, 7–8.

Grossfield, S (1997) *Lost Futures: Our Forgotten Children*. New York: Aperture Foundation.

Gura, P (1992) *Exploring Learning: Young Children and Blockplay*. London: Paul Chapman Publishing.

Harrist, AW and Bradley, DJ (2003) 'You can't say you can't play: Intervening in the process of social exclusion in the kindergarten classroom', *Early Childhood Research Quarterly*, 18, 185–205.

Health Education Authority (1998) *Young and active? A policy framework of young people and health enhancing physical activity*. London: Health Education Authority.

Hendy, L and Whitebread, D (2000) 'Interpretations of independent learning in the early years', *International Journal of Early Years Education*, 8, 3, 243–252.

Henniger, ML (1995) 'Play: Antidote for childhood stress', *Early Child Development and Care*, 105, 7–12.

Herron, RE and Sutton-Smith, B (1971) *Child's Play*. New York: John Wiley and Sons Inc.

Hestenes, LL and Carroll, DE (2000) 'The play interactions of young children with and without disabilities: Individual and environmental influences', *Early Childhood Research Quarterly*, 15, 2, 229–246.

Hewett, VM (2001) 'Examining the Reggio Emilia approach to early childhood education', *Early Childhood Education Journal*, 29, 2, 95–100.

HM Treasury (2004) *Choice for parents, the best start for children, a ten year strategy for Childcare*. The Stationery Office.

Hohmann, M and Weikart, DP (1995) *Educating Young Children*. Ypsilanti, MI: High/Scope Research Foundation.

Holland, P (2003) *We don't Play with Guns Here*. Buckingham: Open University Press.

Hughes, B (2001) *Evolutionary Playwork and Reflective Analytical Practice*. London and New York: Routledge.

Hutt, C (1979) *Play in the Under-fives: Form, development and function*. Unpublished manuscript.

Hutt, SJ, Tyler, S, Hutt, C and Christopherson, H (1989) *Play, Exploration and Learning: A Natural History of the Preschool.* London and New York: Routledge.

Isaacs, S (1932) *The Children We Teach.* London: University of London Press.

Isenberg, J and Quisenberry, N (2002*) Play: Essential For All Children.* Olney, ML: Association for Childhood Education International.

Ladd, GW and Coleman, CC (1990) 'Young children's peer relationships: Forms, features and functions', in Spodeck, B (ed) *Handbook of Research on the Education of Young Children.* New York, NY: Macmillan Publishing Company.

Laine, K and Neitola, M (2004) *Teachers' Opinions and Parents' Ideas About the Social Behaviour, Personality Traits and Play Interactions of the Children With Multiple Problems in Peer Interactions.* Paper presented at the European Conference on Educational Research, University of Crete, 22–25 September.

Langsted, O (1994) 'Looking at quality from the child's perspective', in Moss, P and Pence, A (eds) *Valuing Quality in Early Childhood Services.* London: Paul Chapman Publishing.

Lansdown, G and Lancaster, P (2001) Promoting children's welfare by respecting their rights', in Pugh, G (ed) *Contemporary Issues in the Early Years: Working Collaboratively for Children.* London: Paul Chapman Publishing.

Lawrence, E (1952) *Frederick Froebel and English Education.* London: University of London Press.

Lewis, M (1998) 'Changing a playground and its culture', *Education,* 26, 3, 3–13.

Liebschner, J (1991) *Foundations of Progressive Practice The History of the National Froebel Society.* Cambridge: The Lutterworth Press.

Lindon, J (2003) *Too Safe for Their Own Good? Helping Children Learn About Risk and Life Skills.* London: National Early Years Network.

Lous, AM, de Wit, AM, Bruyn, EEJ, Risken-Walraven, JM and Rost, H (2000) 'Depression and play in early childhood: Play behaviour of depressed and non-depressed 3 to 6 year olds in various play situations', *Journal of Emotional and Behavioural Disorders,* Winter, Vol 8, 4, 249–260.

Lous, AM, de Wit, AM, Bruyn, EEJ and Riksen-Walraven, JM (2002) 'Depression markers in young children's play: A comparison between depressed and non-depressed 3 to 6 year olds in various play situations', *Journal of Child Psychology and Psychiatry,* 43, 8, 1029–1038.

Maccoby, E (1990) 'Gender as a social category', in Chess, S and Hertzig, M (eds) *Annual Progress in Child Psychiatry and Child Development*. New York: Brunner.

Maccoby, E and Jacklin, C (1987) 'Sex segregation in childhood', in Reese, H (ed) *Advances in Child Behaviour and Development*. Orlando, FL: Academic Press.

Malaguzzi, L (1994) 'Your image of the child', *Child Care Information Exchange*, 3, 52–61.

Martin, C and Fabes, R (2001) 'The stability and consequences of young children's same-sex peer interactions' *Developmental Psychology*, 37, 431–446.

Meins, E, Fernyhough, C, Fradley, E and Tuckey, M (2001) 'Rethinking maternal sensitivity: Mothers' comments on infants' mental processes predict security of attachment at 12 months', *Journal of Child Psychological Psychiatry*, 42, 5, 637–648.

Mental Health Foundation (1999) *Bright Futures, Promoting Children and Young People's Mental Health*. London: Mental Health Foundation.

Ministry of Education (1996) *Te Whariki Early Childhood Curriculum*. Wellington, New Zealand: Learning Media.

Missuna, C and Pollock, N (1991) 'Play deprivation in children with physical disabilities: The role of the occupational therapist in preventing secondary disability', *The American Journal of Disability*, 45, 10, 882–888.

Moyles, J (2005) *The Excellence of Play* (second edition). Buckingham: Open University Press.

Moyles, J, Adams, S and Musgrove, A (2002) *SPEEL: Study of Pedagogical Effectiveness in Early Learning*. Research Report 363. London: DfES.

National Playing Fields Association (2000) *Best Play: What Play Provision Should Do For Children*. London: NPFA/Children's Play Council/PLAYLINK.

Newell, P (1993) *The UN Convention and Children's Rights in the UK*. London: National Children's Bureau.

NICHD Early Child Care Research Network (1996) 'Characteristics of infant child care: Factors contributing to positive care-giving', *Early Childhood Research Quarterly*, 8, 77–97.

O'Brien, J and Smith, J (2002) 'Childhood transformed? Risk perceptions and the decline of free play', *British Journal of Occupational Therapy*, 65, 3, 123–128.

Olson, SL (1992) 'Development of conduct problems and peer rejection in preschool children: A social systems analysis', *Journal of Abnormal Child Psychology*, 20, 327–350.

Opie, I (1993) *The People in the Playground.* Oxford: Oxford University Press.

Osborn, AF and Milbank, JE (1987) *The Effects of Early Education: A Report from the Child Health and Education Study.* Oxford: Clarendon Press.

Ostrov, J and Keating, C (2004) 'Gender differences in preschool aggression during free play and structured interactions: An observational study', *Social Development*, 13, 2, 255–277.

Ouvry, M (2003) *Exercising Muscles and Minds: Outdoor Play and the Early Years Curriculum.* London: National Children's Bureau.

Paley, VG (1988) *Bad Guys Don't Have Birthdays: Fantasy Play at Four.* Chicago, IL: The University of Chicago Press.

Paley, VG (1992) *You Can't Say You Can't Play.* Cambridge, MA: Harvard University Press.

Parten, MB (1933) 'Social play among preschool children', *Journal of Abnormal and Social Psychology*, 28, 136–147.

Pellegrini, A and Galda, L (1993) 'Ten years after: A re-examination of symbolic play and literacy research', *Reading Research Quarterly*, 28, 163–175.

Piaget, J (1971) 'The theory of stages in cognitive development' in Green, DM, Ford, M and Flamer, G (eds) *Measurement and Piaget.* New York: McGraw-Hill.

Piaget, J (1985) 'Symbolic play' in Bruner, JS, Jolly, A and Sylva, K (eds) *Play: Its Role in Development and Evolution.* Harmondsworth: Penguin Books.

Plato (360 BCE) *Laws*, translated by Benjamin Jowett. New York: Basic Books.

Plato (1955) *The Republic*, translated by HD Lee. Harmondsworth: Penguin.

Pugh, G (2005) 'Policy matters' in Abbott, L and Langston, A (eds) *Birth to Three: Matters Supporting the Framework of Effective Practice.* Buckingham: Open University Press.

Qualifications and Curriculum Authority (2000) *Curriculum Guidance For the Foundation Stage.* London: QCA Publications.

Raymond, A and Raymond, S (2000) *Children in War.* New York: TV Books.

Reddy, V and Trevarthen, C (2004) 'What we learn about babies from engaging with their emotions', *Zero to Three,* January, 3, 9–15.

Rich, D (2003) 'BANG! BANG! Gun play and why children need it', *Early Education,* Summer, 1–5.

Rousseau, J (1762/1963) *Emile.* London: Everyman.

Rutter, J (2002) *Educating Asylum Seeking and Refugee Children.* London: Department for Education and Skills.

Rutter, M (1972) *Maternal Deprivation Reassessed.* Harmondsworth: Penguin Books.

Sandberg, A and Pramling-Samuelson, I (2005) 'An interview study of gender differences in preschool teachers' attitudes towards children's play', *Early Childhood Education Journal,* 32, 5, 297–305.

Santer, J (2000) *Young Children First Implementing the High/Scope Curriculum in Four Preschool Settings.* Newcastle: The University of Newcastle/High/Scope UK.

Saracho, ON and Spodek, B (1998) *Multiple Perspectives on Play in Early Childhood Education.* New York: State University of New York Press.

Schaffer, HR (1971) *The Growth of Sociability.* Baltimore: Penguin Books.

School Curriculum and Assessment Authority (1996) *Desirable Outcomes for Children's Learning on Entering Compulsory Education,* Department for Education and Employment and School Curriculum and Assessment Authority.

Schweinhart, LS and Weikart, DP (1997) *The High/Scope Preschool Curriculum Comparison Study Through Age 23.* Ypsilanti, MI: High/Scope Press.

Scott, J (2000) 'Children as respondents', in James, A and Christensen, P (eds) *Research With Children: Perspectives and Practices* (pp.98–119). Falmer, Sussex: Falmer Press.

Selleck, D (2001) 'Being under 3 years of age: Enhancing quality experiences', in Pugh, G (ed) *Contemporary Issues in the Early Years: Working Collaboratively for Children.* London: Paul Chapman Publishing.

Serbin, LA, Tonick, IJ and Sternglanz, SH (1977) 'Shaping co-operative cross-sex play', *Child Development,* 48, 924–929.

Siraj-Blatchford, I (2001) 'Diversity and learning in the early years', in Pugh, G (ed) *Contemporary Issues in the Early Years: Working Collaboratively for Children.* London: Paul Chapman Publishing.

Siraj-Blatchford, I (2005) *Evaluation of the Implementation of Foundation Phase Project Across Wales.* London: Institute of Education.

Siraj-Blatchford, J and Siraj-Blatchford, I (2002) 'Discriminating between schemes and schemas in young children's emergent learning of science and technology', *International Journal of Early Years Education,* 10, 3, 205–214.

Stephenson, A (2003) Physical risk-taking: Dangerous or endangered?' *Early Years,* 23, 1, 35–43.

Stoller, SA, Dye Collins, PA and Barnett, DW (1994) 'Structured free play to reduce disruptive activity changes in a Head Start classroom', *School Psychology Review,* 23, 2, 310–322.

Street, C (2002) 'Play and education', *Highlight, 195. National Children's Bureau.*

SureStart (2003) *Birth to Three Matters: A Framework to Support Children in Their Earliest Years.* Norwich: The Stationery Office.

Sutton-Smith, B (1979) *Play and Learning.* New York: Gardener Press, Inc.

Sutton-Smith, B (1997) *The Ambiguity of Play.* Cambridge MA: Harvard University Press.

Sylva, K (1994) 'The impact of early learning on children's later development', in Ball, C (ed) *Start Right: The Importance of Early Learning.* London: Royal Society for the Encouragement of the Arts, Manufacturers and Commerce.

Sylva, K (1997) 'The quest for quality in curriculum', in Schweinhart, LS and Weikart, DP (eds) *The High/Scope Preschool Curriculum Comparison Study Through Age 23.* Ypsilanti, MI: High/Scope Press.

Sylva, K, Siraj-Blatchford, I, Melhuish, E, Sammons, P and Taggart, B (1999) *Effective Provision for Preschool Education Project: Technical Paper 6.* London: DfEE and Institute of Education, University of London.

Sylva, K, Siraj-Blatchford, I, Melhuish, E Sammons, P and Taggart, B (2004) *Effective Provision for Preschool Education Project: Final Report.* London: DfEE and Institute of Education, University of London.

Teacher Training Agency (2003) *Qualifying to Teach: Handbook of Guidance.* London: TTA.

Thomas, N and Smith, C (2004) 'Developing play skills in children with autistic spectrum disorders', *Educational Psychology in Practice,* 20, 3, 195–206.

Tizard, B and Hughes, M (1984) *Young Children Learning.* London: Fontana.

Tizard, B, Blatchford, P, Burke, J, Farquar, C and Plewis, I (1988) *Young Children at School in the Inner City.* Hillsdale, NJ: Lawrence Erlbaum Associates.

Trevarthen, C (2005) 'First things first', *Journal of Child Psychiatry*, 31, 1, 91–113.

Tweed, J (1999) 'Children must be able to play outside says charity', *Nursery World*, 99 (3673).

Utting, D, Bright, J and Hendricson, C (1993) *Crime and the Family: Improving Child-rearing and Preventing Delinquency*. London: Family Policy Unit.

Vygotsky, LS (1962) *Thought and Language*. Cambridge MA: MIT Press.

Vygotsky, LS (1978) *Mind in Society: The Development of Higher Psychological Processes*. Cambridge, MA: Harvard University Press.

Welsh Assembly Government (2006) *Wales Play Policy Implementation*, February, Cardiff.

Welshman (1997) cited in Bailey, R (1999) 'Play, health and physical development', in Moyles, J (ed) *Young Children Learning*. London: Paul Chapman Publishing.

Whitebread, D, Coltman, P, Anderson, H, Sanjana, M and Pino Pasternack, D (2005) *Metacognition in Young Children: Evidence From a Naturalistic Study of 3–5 Year Olds*. Symposium Paper, University of Cyprus, Nicosia.

Wolfberg, P (1999) *Play and Imagination in Children with Autism*. New York: Teachers' College Press.

Wolfendale, S (2001) 'Meeting special needs in the early years', in Pugh, G (ed) *Contemporary Issues in the Early Years: Working Collaboratively for Children* (third edition). London: Paul Chapman Publishing.

Wood, E and Attfield, J (1996) *Play, Learning and the Early Childhood Curriculum*. London: Paul Chapman Publishing.

Alderson, P (1995) *Listening to Children: Children, Ethics and Social Research.* Barkingside: Barnardo's.

Berger, J (1972) *Ways of Seeing.* Harmondsworth: Penguin.

Berk, L and Winsler, A (1995) *Scaffolding Children's Learning: Vygotsky and Early Childhood Education.* Washington, DC: National Association for the Education of Young Children.

Beyer, J and Gammeltoft, L (2000) *Autism and Play.* London: J Kingsley.

Brierley, J (1980) *Children's Well-Being.* Slough: National Foundation for Educational Research.

Brindle, D (1999) 'Eight in ten parents see strangers as risk', *The Guardian,* 4 August 2002.

Bruce, T (1987) *Early Childhood Education.* London: Hodder and Stoughton.

Bruce, T (1992) Time to Play in Early Childhood Education. London: Hodder and Stoughton.

Chandler, T (2006) *The Development of Government Policy in Early Years Leading to the Establishment of Children's Centres.* Briefing paper for The National Professional Qualification in Integrated Centre Leadership Programme.

Cloke, P and Jones, O (2005) 'Unclaimed territory: Childhood and disordered spaces', *Social and Cultural Geography,* 6, 3, 311.

Cole, DA and Carpentieri, S (1990) 'Social status and the co-morbidity of child depression and conduct disorder', *Journal of Consulting and Clinical Psychology,* 58, 748–757.

Cole-Hamilton, I, Harrop, A and Street, C (2002) *Making the Case for Play: Gathering the Evidence.* London: Children's Play Council.

Dishman, RK (1986) 'Mental health', in Seefeld, V (ed) *Physical Activity and Well-being,* Retson, VA: AAHPERD.

Dweck, CS (1999a) 'Caution – praise can be dangerous', *American Educator,* 23(1), 4–9.

Dweck, CS (1999b) *Self-theories: Their Role in Motivation, Personality and Development.* Philadelphia, PA: Psychology Press.

Fineberg, A (1997) *The Innocent Eye: Children's Art and the Modern Artist.* Princeton: Princeton University Press.

Graue, ME and Walsh, DJ (1998) *Studying Children In Context: Theories, Methods and Ethics.* London: Sage.

Gruber, JJ (1986) 'Physical activity and self esteem development in children: A meta-analysis', in Stull, GA and Eckert, HM (eds) *Effects of Physical Activity on Children.* Champaign, IL: Human Kinetics.

Haight, W and others (1999) 'Universal, developmental and variable aspects of young children's play', *Child Development,* 70, 6, 1477–1488.

Hyder, T (2004) *War, Conflict and Play.* Buckingham: Open University Press.

Isaacs, S (1968) *The Nursery Years.* London: Routledge and Kegan Paul.

Jowett, S and Sylva, K (1986) 'Does kind of preschool matter?', *Educational Research,* 28, 1, 21–23.

Kampmann (2001) *Hvad er bornekultur? i: Bornekultur Hvilke born? Og hvis kultur?* Sekretariat for Bornekulturnetvaerk, Akademisk.

Kielhofner, G (1995) *A Model Of Human Occupation: Theory and Application* (second edition). Baltimore, ML: Williams and Wilkers.

Kopp, CB, Baker, BL and Brown, KW (1992) 'Social skills and their correlates: Preschoolers with developmental delays', *American Journal on Mental Retardation,* 96, 4, 357–366.

Lewis, A and Lindsay, G (eds) (2000) *Researching Children's Perspectives.* Buckingham: Open University Press.

Liebschner, J (1992) *A Child's Work: Freedom and Guidance in Froebel's Educational Theory and Practice.* Cambridge: The Lutterworth Press.

Malaguzzi, L (1993) 'History, ideas and basic philosophy', in Edwards, C, Gandani, L and Forman, G (1998) *The Hundred Languages of Children.* New York: Norwood.

Manning-Morton, J and Thorp, M (2004) *Key Times for Play.* Buckingham: Open University Press.

Mayall, B (1994) 'Children in action at home and school', in Mayall, B (ed) *Children's Childhoods Observed and Experienced.* Falmer, Sussex: Falmer Press.

McTaggart, R (ed) (1997) *Participatory Action Research.* New York: Albany.

Nabuco, M and Sylva, K (1996) *Comparisons Between Ecers Ratings and Individual Preschool Centres and the Results of Target Child Observations: Do They Match Or Do They Differ?* Paper presented to the 5th European Conference on the Quality of Early Childhood Education, Paris.

Nutbrown, C (2006) *Key Concepts in Early Childhood Education and Care.* Newbury Park, CA: Sage Publications.

Nutbrown, C and Hannon, P (2003) 'Children's perspectives on family literacy: Methodological issues, findings and implications for practice', *Journal of Early Childhood Literacy,* 3, 2, 115–145.

O'Kane, C (2000) 'The development of participatory techniques: Facilitating children's views about decisions which affect them', in Christensen, P and James, A (eds) *Research With Children: Perspectives and Practices* (pp.136–159). Falmer, Sussex: Falmer Press.

Oliver, M (1992) 'Changing the social relations of research production', *Disability, Handicap and Society*, 7, 2, 101–114.

Pellegrini, A and Smith, P (1998) 'The development of play during childhood: Forms and possible functions', *Child Psychology and Psychiatry Review*, 3, 2, 58–67.

Piaget, J (1962) *Play, Dreams and Imitation in Childhood*. London: Routledge and Kegan Paul.

Priestley, M (1998) 'Childhood disability and disabled childhoods: Agendas for research' *Childhood*, 5, 2, 207–223.

Schaeffer, CE (1993) *The Therapeutic Powers of Play*. Northvale, NJ: Jason Aronson.

Schaffer, HR (1996) *Social Development*. Oxford: Blackwell Publishing.

Schweinhart, LJ, and Weikart, DP (1986) *Significant Benefits: The High/Scope Perry Preschool Study Through Age 27*. Ypsilanti, MI: High/Scope Press.

Smilansky, S (1986) *The Effects of Socio-Dramatic Play on Disadvantaged Preschool Children*. New York: John Wiley.

Sutton-Smith, B and Kelly-Byrne, D (1984) 'The idealization of play', in Smith, PK (ed) *Play in Animals and Humans*. Oxford: Basil Blackwell.

Swain, J and French, S (1998) 'A voice in what? Researching the lives and experiences of visually disabled people', in Barton, L and Clough, P (eds) *Articulating with Difficulty: Researching Voices in Inclusive Education*. London: Paul Chapman Publishing.

Trevarthen, C (1980) 'The foundations of intersubjectivity', in Olson, D (ed) *The Social Foundations of Language and Thought*. New York: Norton.

Trevarthen, C (2001) *Tuning in to Children: Motherese and Teacherese, the Listening Voice*. Paper given at Pen Green Centre, 24 March.

Wadsworth, BJ (1989) *Piaget's Theory of Cognitive and Affective Development* (fourth edition). New York and London: Longman.

Whitburn, J (2003) 'Learning to live together: The Japanese model of early years education', *International Journal of Early Years Education*, 11, 2, 155–175.

Winnicott, DW (1982) *Playing and Reality*. Harmondsworth: Penguin Education.